The Christmas Eve Cookbook

The Christmas

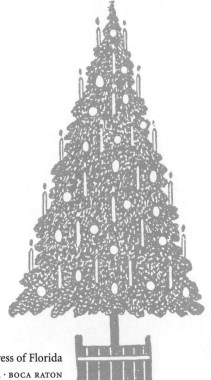

University Press of Florida

GAINESVILLE · TALLAHASSEE · TAMPA · BOCA RATON

PENSACOLA · ORLANDO · MIAMI · JACKSONVILLE

Eve Cookbook

With Tales of Nochebuena and Chanukah

Ferdie Pacheco and Luisita Sevilla Pacheco

03 02 01 00 99 98 6 5 4 3 2 1

LIBRARY OF CONGRESS CATALOGING-IN-PUBLICATION DATA
Pacheco, Ferdie.
The Christmas Eve cookbook: with tales of Nochebuena and Chanukah /
Ferdie Pacheco and Luisita Sevilla Pacheco.
p. cm.
Includes bibliographical references and index.
ISBN 0-8130-1624-X (alk. paper)
1. Christmas cookery. 2. Hanukkah cookery. 3. Holiday cookery. 4. Cookery,
International. 5. Holidays—Fiction. I. Sevilla, Luisita. II. Title.
TX739.2.C45P33   1998
641.5'68—dc21   98-15243

Publisher's Note: The reader is advised to follow standard practices of safe food handling whenever preparing meals at home. The publisher is not responsible for the failure of the reader to take such precautions.

The University Press of Florida is the scholarly publishing agency for
the State University System of Florida, comprising Florida A & M University, Florida
Atlantic University, Florida International University, Florida State University,
University of Central Florida, University of Florida, University of North Florida,
University of South Florida, and University of West Florida.

University Press of Florida
15 Northwest 15th Street
Gainesville, FL 32611
http://nersp.nerdc.ufl.edu/~upf

We dedicate this cookbook to the women who contributed their holiday recipes, and to the mothers and grandmothers of Ybor City, who were the master chefs of our time.

Contents

Recipes

Acknowledgments

In writing a cookbook of this scope it was necessary to call upon a variety of friends, neighbors, experts, and other cookbook authors. Luisita and I hope to list here all of those who have contributed to the completeness of this book, and if we have omitted your name, it was purely unintentional. Forgive us.

The greatest contribution to this book was that of Marina Polvay, author of twelve cookbooks and host of several TV and radio shows, a woman with several lifetimes of experience in the kitchen. "International" is the word that best describes Marina, the daughter of Prince Konstantine Sherbatoff and Countess Eugenia Szenutovits Berezsny Sherbatoff of Russia; she lived in a turbulent era of revolution and traveled all over Europe, living in Siberia, Ukraine, Hungary, and Austria before settling at last in the United States.

Of inestimable help has been Adela Hernandez Gonzmart, coauthor of our first cookbook, *The Columbia Restaurant Cookbook*. We particularly thank Adela, Mary Alessi, and Susan Pérez for their contributions to the "Holiday Melting Pot" chapter. Our thanks also to Aziza Mansour, who spent hours learning our computer system and typing the manuscript. For the contribution of their stories, recipes, and some of our fondest memories, our heartfelt thanks go to the following.

To our Spanish friends and family, including Adela Hernandez Gonzmart, Consuelo Pacheco, Carmen Jimenez, Teresa Kaplan, Antonia Palacios, Mariano Parra and Aurora Esparsa, we say *Feliz Nochebuena*—and the same to our Cuban friends and family members Teresa Fernandez (Malaga Restaurant), Bobby Rodriguez, Vera Dubson, Ana Torres, and Aida Stable.

To our Mexican-American relatives, friends, and neighbors—Luisita's mother, Margo Maestas, Mike Maestas, Orlando Trujillo, Barbara Jean Vigil, Brian and Dean Vigil, Mary Gailhouse, Rita Couch, Kit Croell, Josie Trujillo, Inocencia Galindo, Katie Galindo, and Lottie Kimball—we say *muchas gracias* and *Feliz Navidad.*

To American family of multiethnic (or indeterminate!) ancestry, Pamela McLaughlin, Kelly Landry, Kim Egelsten, Bernadette Cunningham, Kathi and Dave Gomendi, and Tina Pacheco, our thanks and a happy Christmas Eve.

To Italian friends Ermanno Perrotti (Da Ermanno Restaurant, Miami), Mary Alessi, Buster Agliano, Frank Accurso, Phil Alessi, Rosalie Perrone, Consuelo Mafalda, Rosalie Irene, Nana Rose, Jean Lala, Francesco and Maria Rametta, Dana Perone, Tony Rametta, Fifi Ciaccio, and Angie La Salvia—*grazie* and *buon Natale!*

And finally, to the Jewish friends, old and new, who made the Chanukah section of this book possible—Pauline Winick, Natalie Kleinberg, Doris Chaite Rosenblatt, Adrienne Teufeld, Barbara Manning, Frances Leiderman, Sarah Wolf, Mimi Roth, Jallele, and Joy Gilman—a very happy Chanukah.

A Holiday Melting Pot

by Ferdie Pacheco

Before my wife, Luisita, takes you into the kitchen to cook up a storm of holiday dishes—and before I let you settle into a comfy chair by the fire to enjoy this collection of holiday stories—let us tell you a little about how this book came to be.

In many ethnic-American families, Christmas Eve—in Spanish, *Nochebuena* (the Good Night), in Italian, *La Vigilia di Natale*—is the primary feast day of the winter season. In American-Jewish families, of course, Chanukah is celebrated.

I grew up in Ybor City, an immigrant neighborhood in Tampa, Florida, and in the 1930s and '40s, it was a wonderful example of the American melting pot at work—only, of course, nothing ever really "melted." Ybor City was composed predominantly of Cuban, Italian, Spanish, and Jewish immigrants, all of whom worked side by side in Tampa's cigar factories and mercantile establishments, but none of whom celebrated their December feast day in quite the same way. Each group had its own unique holiday traditions, and each one set a different holiday table, depending on the customs of their respective homelands.

While our holiday traditions changed in the New World, they certainly did not mirror the Anglo experience of Christmas, which centered around Christmas Day rather than Christmas Eve. Nor did we ever eat "turkey with all the trimmings." In many Latin families, gifts weren't even exchanged until January 6, the Day of the Wise Men, otherwise known as the Epiphany. Even today, the modern-day descendants of immigrant families still practice and cherish their own unique holiday customs.

Lots of the stories and recipes that make up this book come from my early childhood years in Ybor City. In keeping with the melting pot theme, however, I have added some modern-day stories that were just too good to pass up, each of which demonstrates the wonderful variety of holiday celebrations that still exists in America.

Like salt to the soup, we've also added the culinary joys of Mexican cuisine which, while not well known in Ybor City, were a part of the holiday menu of my own family (the Spanish Jimenez clan), the taste for which they acquired during their years spent in Mexico prior to the Revolution of 1910. What's more, Luisita, the culinary expert of this book, is of Mexican-Apache-Spanish stock and from a family, the Maestas clan of Denver, that traces its lineage back several centuries in the Southwest. Mexican food was a natural part of our own Nochebuena celebration, so naturally it's included here.

And that's what the Holiday Melting Pot is all about—bringing together the wonderful variety and treasury of unique ethnic foods and customs without trying to force them to jell into a single Christmas Jell-O mold. In reality there are as many different holiday traditions in this country as there are families—and *that* is the beauty and legacy of our American immigrant experience. Some of the recipes on our list have no ethnic roots—and the only reason they're included in a particular ethnic group is that they came from an Italian chef, a Cuban lady, etc. So we make no apology for the breadth and scope of the recipes and *cuentos* (tales) of Nochebuena,

Christmas Eve, and Chanukah in this book. Good food and good stories know no boundaries of time or place. Many of the tales told here date so far back as to be unverifiable. I must ask the reader to show some good holiday spirit, indulge an old storyteller, and not be too critical.

But first, a sampling of some of the holiday customs and history represented in this book, and some typical menus on the holiday tables of the various ethnic groups in Ybor City, beginning with what in the end may be that of the minority—an "All-American" Christmas.

AN AMERICAN
CHRISTMAS EVE DINNER

Salmon Mousse
Rib Roast
Roasted Potatoes
Asparagus Tips with
    Hollandaise Sauce
Black Cherry
    and Cranberry Mold
Caesar Salad
Apple Pie

AN AMERICAN
CHRISTMAS DAY DINNER

Relish Tray
Turkey with Stuffing and
Giblet Gravy
Baked Country Ham
Candied Sweet Potatoes
Mashed Potatoes
Mixed Green Salad
Cranberry Relish
Lime Bavarian Mold
Pumpkin Pie
Mincemeat Pie

Chanukah in Ybor City

After I had finished writing my third book on Ybor City, I found I had committed a grievous oversight. Nowhere had I remembered the Jewish people of Ybor City. I was shocked by my oversight, and the more I thought about it, the more bewildered I became at my egregious omission of what was a significant part of my young life in Ybor City. Our Chanukah stories and recipes are dedicated to Doris Chaite Rosenblatt, for whose help and assistance we are deeply appreciative.

Florida's Jewish population dates back to 1763, when Spain assumed control of the Louisiana territory. The memory of the Spanish Inquisition still a strong part of their shared history, the large community of Sephardic Jews in New Orleans fled to other territories, including La Florida, which had just been taken from the Spanish by the British. In 1783, La Florida reverted to Spanish rule, but had so few Jewish residents that they were largely ignored. By 1845, when Florida became a state, the Jewish population numbered fewer than 100 families. With the influx of immigrants to America in the late nineteenth century, Ybor City's Jewish population grew, many coming from Romania and other parts of eastern Europe.

Politically and economically, the Jews of Ybor City were aligned with the Cubans' fight for independence from Spain. In November of 1892, a man named Edward Steinberg introduced José Martí to various Jewish community groups in Ybor, who then donated their entire treasuries to the cause of Cuban freedom. There was, of course, prejudice and conflict among Ybor City's ethnic groups, but for the most part, Sicilians, Cubans, Spaniards, and Jews worked together to help each other survive in the New World.

So, while my critics may well carp that a menu of Chanukah delicacies has no place in a Christmas Eve cookbook, I disagree. While my family was celebrating Nochebuena, our Jewish neighbors were celebrating Chanukah, and the inclusion of their recipes in an Ybor City holiday cookbook is entirely appropriate.

On the 25th day of Kislev in the Jewish calendar, Jews throughout the world light the first Chanukah candle. One of the minor Jewish festivals, Chanukah commemorates the Maccabean victory over Antiochus IV of Syria twenty-one centuries ago. Though heavily outnumbered by the Syrians, the Jews were spurred into action by Mattathias and his sons, especially Judah Maccabeus. They defeated the Assyrians to regain control of the Temple, which had been Hellenized and defiled.

During the ritual cleansing of the Temple, the priests found only enough oil to burn for one day. But, miraculously, the one-day supply of oil lasted for eight days. So today, on each of the eight nights of Chanukah, a candle is lit, until on the last night all eight are burning.

After the lighting of the candles, it is traditional to sing songs, play a game with a dreidel (a spinning top), open presents, and eat latkes (potato pancakes) and other holiday foods.

The history of the latke in particular deserves special note (primarily because it is my favorite of all Chanukah foods). In the North African Jewish tradition, latkes are an older part of the Chanukah celebration. Sephardic families, descended from European Jews, cannot trace the latke back as far, because potatoes were not available to them until the sixteenth century, when they were brought from Peru and Bolivia.

The symbolism of the pancake is threefold. Initially made of flour and water, it serves as a reminder of the plain food taken into battle by the Maccabees. The oil in which latkes are prepared symbolizes the cleansing and rededication of the Temple after it was defiled by the Assyrians. The third aspect of the pancake's symbolism was not added until medieval times, when it was said to also symbolize the food Judith served to the Assyrian general Holofernes before she cut off his head.

Originally Chanukah was merely a solstice commemoration of the Maccabean saga. It wasn't until the Middle Ages that it evolved from a distinctly minor Temple holiday into a relatively significant family celebration.

MENU FOR CHANUKAH

Mushroom Barley Soup
Stuffed Breast of Veal or Fruited Pot Roast
Latkes

Kugel (Noodle Pudding)
Applesauce
Honey Cake

An Italian Christmas Eve

For Italians, the Christmas season begins eight days before December 25 and lasts until Twelfth Night, or Epiphany, on January 6. On December 23 (and often earlier), children dressed as shepherds, in sandals and rustic hats, go from door to door singing songs and giving recitations called *pastóráles,* thus reenacting the journey of the shepherds to the Nativity manger.

First popularized by Saint Francis at Gréccio in 1224, the *presèpio,* or Nativity scene, is an important part of the Italian Christmas celebration in both the home and the church. These displays are often quite elaborate, including not only the Christ Child, Holy Family, and Three Wise Men, but the entire city of Bethlehem. The making of *presèpi* became a popular art in Italy, and churches often vied with each other to have the best one. Even today, the Nativity scene is the most cherished Christmas display for many Italians, in spite of the competing presence, particularly in America, of the Christmas tree.

In the old days, in Italy and in immigrant neighborhoods like Ybor City, the children had to bide their time until January 6, which marked the coming of the Three Wise Men bearing gifts. In parts of Italy, including Sicily, the benevolent witch La Befana brought gifts of toys and sweets, which she left in children's stockings. In some traditions, La Befana carries a switch and lumps of coal for mischievous children. As the story goes, Befana came by her job because she refused to help the Three Wise Men, who stopped to ask her the way to Bethlehem. After sending them away, Befana repented and tried to find them. Every year she continues her search, rewarding good children and punishing the bad along the way. In modern-day America, Befana is all but forgotten. The most pragmatic of creatures, children today wait for Santa Claus, who gets their gifts to them thirteen days sooner!

Many Italian families, and Sicilians in particular, fast from sunset on December 23 until sunset on December 24. To break the fast, a great Christmas log is kindled, prayers are said around the *presèpio*, and then, before Midnight Mass, the feast begins. The variety of foods is endless, but often it includes *capitóne* (eels), pasta, fish, sweet pastries and breads, and nougat candy.

In Ybor City the Italians, most of whom spoke Spanish, referred to Christmas Eve interchangeably as Nochebuena and La Vigilia di Natale. It was difficult to say what a typical Italian Christmas Eve feast consisted of, because there were both Sicilians and mainland Italians. For the most part, however, Italians had fish on Christmas Eve, owing in part to the dietary restrictions of the Catholic Church, which prohibited the eating of meat on Fridays and on certain holidays, including Christmas Eve. (The Spanish, on the other hand, had received a special dispensation from the Church as reward for their expulsion of the Moors, and were allowed to eat meat!) In Ybor City it seemed that Sicilians preferred fish, whereas mainland Italians generally also had meat or fowl.

The night began with appetizers, including *caponata* (pickled eggplant), sausage, cheese, and *olivi scacciate* (cracked olive salad). Most Italians served a homemade red wine with the dinner. It was made in October and the cask was opened in December for Christmas Eve. In this they differed from Ybor City's Spaniards and Cubans, who favored bottled red and white wines from Europe.

Many of Ybor City's immigrant families cooked on an igloo-shaped brick oven or on a *forno* (a large, bucket-shaped furnace elevated on bricks) in their backyards. The first course of the meal was often a small plate of soup, usually minestrone (made with fresh vegetables) or chicken broth with *cappellini*.

A pasta dish always followed. The type of pasta varied, but the sauce was almost always made from canned Italian tomatoes, slow-cooked for three hours. Afterwards, a meat that had been fast-fried to lock in the blood was added along with garlic, onion, and basil and simmered for an hour more.

For most Italians, the main dish on the Nochebuena table was *escabeche,* made with fresh fish, usually red snapper (*pargo*). The fish was gutted and filled with a stuffing made of bits of lobster, shrimp, crab, celery, and condiments. The fish was then sewed up or fastened with toothpicks, basted in a preheated mixture of olive oil, butter, and a pinch of garlic, and served whole. Most in Ybor City agree that turkey was never served, though some Italians did broil chickens and potatoes for the main course, and leg of veal was also popular.

Remembering the ways of the old country, some Italians in Ybor City bought a young goat (*capretto*) each Christmas Eve and cooked it over an open fire in much the same way that Cubans cook their *lechón,* or suckling pig. While the goat rotated on its spit, it was basted with *mojo* sauce, identical to the Cuban version described below, except most Italians added mint.

After the meal, while the women cleared the table, slices of Italian sausage and a sausage-stuffed pastry from Sicily called *brignolata* were served, as were mixed nuts, roasted chestnuts, and small sweets such as *cudureddi di figo, pinulata*, and ricotta triangles. Favorite desserts also included various cakes and pastries such as *cassata, cannoli,* fruit and cheese, and *torróne* and *cubiata* (nougat candies imported from Italy and very similar to the Spanish *turrón*). At last, espresso coffee was served topped with a single coffee bean and a finger of anisette.

While the women cleared the table, the men usually played cards—either *chick netta* (a form of poker), hearts, or straight poker. Those with big-enough yards played bocci, an Italian bowling game, but such yards were few in Ybor City. Later, everyone went to Midnight Mass to welcome and honor the arrival of the Christ Child.

Caponata	Stuffed Flounder
Italian Sausage Pinwheels	Baked Red Snapper
Olive Salad	Baked Fettuccine
Pumpkin Tortellini	White Lasagna
Batter-Fried Vegetables	Ricotta Triangles
Brignolata	Sfingi
Tomato Salad with Basil	Cannoli
Spaghettini in Broth	Sicilian Cake

A Mexican Nochebuena

Beginning nine days before Christmas (commemorating the time it took Mary and Joseph to travel from Nazareth to Bethlehem), Mexicans reenact Mary and Joseph's search for shelter in a procession called *la posada,* which translated literally means "inn" or "place of lodging." From house to house the procession travels, carrying clay and papier-mâché figures of Joseph and Mary. At each house they serenade the owners and ask for shelter, but are turned away—until finally the designated host for the evening lets them enter. Upon being admitted, they light candles and kneel before the Nativity scene (*Nacimiento*), wherein they place the figures of Mary and Joseph and, on Christmas Eve, the Christ Child. Prayers are said, songs sung, and thus the beginning of the feast is signaled. The pilgrims are treated to a vast array of fruits and Mexican traditional dishes, including turkey with mole sauce, empanadas, tamales, chili, beans, rice, and a variety of desserts.

For children the highlight is the breaking of the piñata, a big papier-mâché bird or donkey (or a painted earthenware jar) filled with toys and sweets. Blindfolded, the youngest child is given a stick with which to try and break open the piñata. Each child takes a turn until the contents spill out onto the floor, and all the children scramble for the gifts.

The families then attend Midnight Mass, or *Misa del Gallo* (the Mass of the Rooster), which commemorates the birth of Christ as the only time the cock ever crowed at midnight. Fireworks, bell ringing, music, singing, and even the shooting off of firearms often follow the mass as Christmas Day is ushered in—*Feliz Navidad!*

A MEXICAN NOCHEBUENA DINNER

Menudo	Rice
Tamales	Pinto Beans
Turkey with Mole Sauce	Sopaipillas
Green Chili	Bread Pudding

Spanish and Cuban Nochebuena Customs

Spain and Cuba have very similar Christmas customs, differing primarily in the types of foods consumed. Since Cuba has a richer variety of tropical foods, the Cuban holiday menu tends to be more varied and exotic than that of Spain.

Nochebuena is perhaps the biggest night of celebration for Spanish-speaking people throughout the world. This is the one night during the Christmas holidays that the entire family will gather to celebrate. Because it is the day on which the Holy Family is revered, it is often the holiday set aside for family reunions.

In Spain, the Christmas season begins on December 8, with the Feast of the Immaculate Conception, commemorating Spain's patron saint, the Virgin Mary.

As in Italy, the Christmas tree (when there is one at all) takes second place in Spain to the elaborately made *Beléns* (models of Bethlehem), also called *Nacimientos,* or Nativity displays. Depending on the artistry and resources available in a home, these Nativity scenes are a source of great pride to a Spanish household. In Cuba, because of its close proximity to the United States, Christmas trees were more common, particularly prior to the rule of Castro. No less than the Spaniards, however, Cubans have always built lavish *Beléns* under the tree.

Santa Claus is an outcast in Spain, where the children must wait until January 6, the day of the Three Wise Men, when Melchior, Balthazar, and Gaspar come riding their camels through the city gates, laden with gifts. Again because of their proximity to the United States, Cuban families quickly adopted Santa Claus as the preferred giver of gifts, although there were some families who stuck by the Three Wise Men. The clever offspring of *some* Cuban parents won the day by insisting that both Santa Claus *and* the Three Wise Men visit, thereby illustrating again the wonderful pragmatism and wisdom of children who stand to receive gifts!

In Spanish homes, the Nochebuena feast was divided into courses and began with appetizers like roasted chestnuts, marzipan, *bollinas* (fried turnovers), and *turrón* (nougat). Chicken soup followed, and because Spaniards rarely served salad on Nochebuena, this was immediately followed by the main entree, which was typically roasted chicken and potatoes. Like the Italians of Ybor City, the Spanish often served red snapper, but it was rarely the focal point of the meal. Some families also ate Serrano ham, which is very similar to Italian prosciutto. The favorite dessert was *brazo gitano,* a cream-filled sponge cake covered in a sweet sherry syrup and topped with meringue.

Jamón Serrano and Manchego Cheese
Bollinas
Seafood Salad
Almond Soup
Spanish Red Snapper or Baked Porgy
Stuffed Breast of Turkey, Catalan Style
Roasted Chicken and Potatoes
Yellow Rice
Baked Red Cabbage with Apples
Marzipan
Brazo Gitano
Turrón

Both in mainland Cuba and in Cuban-American homes, the main en-trée for Nochebuena was a suckling pig, or *lechón*, turned and roasted over an open fire. The pig was basted with *mojo*, a sauce made of sour orange juice, garlic, oregano, and bay leaves. Guava leaves were added to the fire for the aroma and flavor they imparted to the roasting pig.

Unlike the Spaniards' Nochebuena, the Cuban feast did not proceed one course at a time, but instead hit with full force all at once, rather like a tropical storm. The Cubans wasted very little time with appetizers or soup. Unique to the Cuban Nochebuena table were plantains, tomato and water-cress salad, black beans and rice (*olla*), and the white, pulpy, delicious veg-etable called yucca, also called cassava, which grows all over Cuba and now widely in Florida. Like the potato, yucca is a root, but quite stringy. When cooked it approximates the consistency of mashed potatoes, but has its own unique texture and taste. It was frequently served with lemon and *mojo*.

Spanish cider, beer, and imported white and red wines from Europe were the beverages of choice, and no Nochebuena table—Spanish or Cuban—ever lacked for fresh-baked bread. Ybor City's bread was the best in the world.

Traditional Nochebuena desserts were also representative of foods abundantly available in Cuba. Guava, cheeses, crackers, chestnuts, almonds, fruit, flan, and *turrón* from Spain were all standard fare. Exclusive to Cuba is *membrillo,* a paste made from quince and served with white cheese.

A CUBAN NOCHEBUENA DINNER

Seafood Croquettes	White Rice with Black Beans
Spanish Bean Soup	Watercress and Tomato Salad
Lechón Asado Vasco	Fried Ripe Plantains
Chicken in Wine Sauce	Bunuelos
Yucca Fritters	Guava Cheesecake

In Spanish and Cuban homes (both in the Old World and in Ybor City), the lavish Nochebuena meal was interrupted by bands of strolling singers, or by the sudden appearance of a *gaitero* (bagpiper), which called for the rapt attention of the diners. Following the serenade, the singers and bagpipers were tipped generously and toasted.

For Spaniards and Cubans, espresso coffee, with or without a side of brandy or anisette liqueur, completed the meal—and no Nochebuena was complete unless the men of the family had their Havana cigars (*puros*).

When the meal was finished, the Spaniards typically embarked on a series of card games or played dominoes until it was time for the family to attend Misa del Gallo (Midnight Mass).

Cuban families, on the other hand, liked to push all of the furniture to the sides of the room and dance rumbas, dansones, or mambos until it was time for church. Old men, who do not dance if they are wise, got out of the way, played dominoes, and smoked away on their Havanas. In Ybor City, it was also customary for the men to go outside and shoot firearms and fireworks into the sky, to the great appreciation of the children present.

Following Midnight Mass, only the most hardy stayed up to have hot chocolate, *churros* (doughnuts), or a nightcap.

All in all, Nochebuena truly was "the good night." In Ybor City, it was the night above all others when we overcame our worries and celebrated our good luck to be healthy and living in America.

PHOTO BY GEORGE SCHIAVONE

Appetizers and Dips

Salmon Mousse

1 6-oz. can salmon, or 1 4-oz. can white tuna in oil (preferably Spanish tuna)
1 10½-oz. can cream of asparagus soup
1 8-oz. package cream cheese
1 cup mayonnaise
1 onion, finely chopped
1 tablespoon unflavored gelatin
Juice from 1 lemon
1 tablespoon water
1 teaspoon orange vegetable coloring

Clean salmon of bones and dark spots; set aside. On low heat, cook soup in a saucepan and add cream cheese, warming until soft. Place mixture in a bowl with mayonnaise, onion, and salmon or tuna. Dissolve gelatin in the water and lemon juice, and pour into bowl. Add coloring. Mix all ingredients in a blender until smooth. Oil a mold, pour in mixture, and refrigerate until set. Serves 10–15 as a dip.

Caponata
(Marinated Eggplant)

2 eggplants
1 teaspoon salt, plus enough for sprinkling
½ cup extra-virgin olive oil
1 onion, finely chopped
3 stalks celery, finely chopped
1 cup canned Italian peeled tomatoes
¼ cup white wine vinegar
1 tablespoon sugar
1 cup green olives
2 tablespoons capers

Cut unpeeled eggplants into small cubes. Sprinkle with salt and let stand 1 hour. Rinse, then dry well. Fry in olive oil and drain on paper towels. In same oil, sauté onion and celery until limp; use more oil if needed. Add tomatoes, vinegar, sugar, salt, olives, capers, and eggplant; simmer 5 minutes. Cool and serve at room temperature with crackers. Will keep in refrigerator 2 weeks. Serves 4.

Brignolata
(Sausage Pastries)

1 lb. bread dough
1 lb. Italian sausage (casing removed)
1 egg, beaten

Roll dough into 18 x 12 inch rectangle. Cut into 6 strips, 3 inches wide and 12 inches long. Divide sausage into 6 equal portions. Spread sausage along length of dough strips, leaving a ¼-inch border of dough on all sides. Roll each strip of dough lengthwise and seal edges by pinching seams. With one finger, hold one end of strip down on a flat surface and coil it around to form concentric circles.

Preheat oven to 350 degrees. Place brignolata on a lightly greased pan and brush with egg. Bake 35 to 40 minutes, until brown. Makes 6 pastries.

Italian Sausage Pinwheels

2 cups all-purpose flour
1 tablespoon baking powder
1 teaspoon salt
¼ cup shortening
⅔ cup milk
1 lb. Italian sausage (remove casing), room temperature
1 egg yolk, beaten

In a bowl, combine flour, baking powder, and salt. Cut in shortening until mixture resembles coarse meal. Add milk. Stir until well blended. Cover and refrigerate at least 1 hour.

Turn dough onto a lightly floured board. Knead lightly 3 or 4 times. Roll dough into an 18 x 12 inch rectangle. Spread sausage over dough, leaving a ½-inch margin of dough on all sides. Roll dough lengthwise, like a jelly roll. Pinch seam and ends to seal.

Beat egg yolk and spread over top of dough with a pastry brush. Cut dough into 1½-inch slices to make pinwheels. Place in rows on a baking sheet. Bake in preheated oven at 350 degrees for 20 minutes, until golden brown. Makes 18 pinwheels.

Batter-Fried Vegetables

1 teaspoon baking powder
⅛ teaspoon white pepper
⅛ teaspoon cayenne
½ cup all-purpose flour
½ teaspoon salt

⅛ teaspoon nutmeg
3 eggs, well beaten
2 tablespoons vegetable oil
8 broccoli florets
8 cauliflower florets

Sift baking powder, pepper, cayenne, flour, salt, and nutmeg into a bowl. Make a well in the center, and stir in eggs and oil slowly. Whip with wire whisk or eggbeater until smooth. Cover and set aside.

In separate pots, boil vegetables in 1 inch of water 8 to 10 minutes, until tender; broccoli is done when it turns bright green. Do not overcook. Remove and drain. Beat batter again until light and creamy. Dip each piece in batter. Fry 3–5 minutes, until puffed and brown; if using a deep fryer, set at 375 degrees. Makes 16 pieces.

Crabmeat Dip

2 tablespoons butter
2 small shallots, finely chopped
1 6-oz. can crabmeat

¼ cup heavy cream
¼ cup whiskey
3 tablespoons catsup

Place butter in a saucepan and sauté shallots until translucent. Add crabmeat and cream, and continue to sauté for 3 minutes. Add whiskey and catsup. Simmer until whiskey evaporates and sauce thickens. Serve with toasted bread cut into triangles. Serves 4 as a dip.

Papas Ali-oli
(Potatoes in Garlic Mayonnaise)

1 lb. red potatoes
2 tablespoons extra-virgin olive oil
6 cloves garlic, finely minced or pressed

1 cup mayonnaise
Salt and pepper to taste
Parsley, chopped, for garnish

Boil potatoes in their jackets until tender. Drain, cool, peel, and cut into thick slices. Mix olive oil, mayonnaise, and garlic until smooth. Combine with potatoes until they are well coated. Salt and pepper to taste. Garnish with parsley.

Seafood Croquettes

1 stick unsalted butter
1 medium onion, finely chopped
1 cup all-purpose flour
2 cups milk, heated
2 eggs, beaten lightly
¼ teaspoon nutmeg

½ teaspoon Tabasco sauce
2 tablespoons dry white wine
½ lb. shrimp, cooked and chopped
½ lb. lobster, cooked and chopped
½ lb. crabmeat, cooked and flaked
Salt and pepper to taste

Melt butter in a skillet. Sauté onion until transparent. Add flour and stir until it forms a ball with butter and onion. Add hot milk and stir until mixture becomes a thick sauce. Beat eggs with nutmeg, Tabasco and wine. Fold into prepared sauce. Add seafood. Season with salt and pepper to taste. Cover and chill. Transfer to a platter.

CROQUETTE PREPARATION

2 cups unseasoned bread crumbs
2 eggs, lightly beaten
Flour
Vegetable oil

Place bread crumbs and beaten eggs in separate bowls. Using a tablespoon, divide seafood mixture into small log shapes. With floured hands, roll each croquette in flour, dip in egg, and coat with bread crumbs. Chill 1 hour. Fry in hot oil 1½ inches deep, turning croquettes until golden. Drain. Makes 36.

Ham or Chicken Croquettes

¼ cup butter
¼ cup all-purpose flour
1 small to medium onion, minced
1 cup milk
2 eggs
1 tablespoon freshly squeezed
  lemon juice
½ cup ham or chicken, cooked and
  ground
Salt and pepper to taste
Fine bread crumbs
Oil for deep frying

Melt butter in a saucepan and blend in flour, onion, and milk, stirring constantly until very thick. Stir in 1 egg beaten with lemon juice. Add ham or chicken. Season with salt and pepper to taste. Pour into shallow dish. Let cool.

Shape mixture into small, plump patties. Chill. Dip into crumbs, then into egg beaten with 2 tablespoons water. Dip again into crumbs and let cool. In a skillet, fry in hot oil until golden brown. Makes 12 to 16 croquettes.

Empanadas de Pollo
(Chicken Turnovers)

CHICKEN FILLING

1 large onion, chopped
¼ cup extra-virgin olive oil
1 teaspoon garlic, chopped
1 8-oz. can tomato sauce
2 bay leaves

1 cup cooked chicken, coarsely chopped
½ cup pimiento-stuffed olives, cut in half
¼ cup raisins
⅛ cup capers
Salt and pepper to taste

In a skillet, sauté onion in olive oil until limp. Add garlic, tomato sauce, and bay leaves. Simmer about 15 minutes. Add chicken and rest of ingredients. Stir well. Cover and cook over low heat 10 minutes. Let cool, or make in advance and refrigerate.

PASTRY DOUGH

2 cups all-purpose flour
1 teaspoon salt
⅓ cup shortening

⅓ cup butter
7 tablespoons ice water
1 egg, lightly beaten with 1 tablespoon water
  (for glaze)

Mix flour and salt. Add shortening and butter. Using fork or pastry blender, mix until dough resembles coarse cornmeal. Add ice water one tablespoon at a time, tossing lightly until dough leaves sides of bowl. Wrap in waxed paper and refrigerate 30 minutes. Cut dough in half and roll with a floured rolling pin into a 9-inch circle. Cut smaller circles with top of a shortening can or any other 4-inch round cutter. Combine leftover fragments and roll out again; repeat with other half of dough.

Place 1 tablespoon of filling in center of each 4-inch circle, moisten edges with cold water, fold over, and press together. Use a fork to crimp edges and prick top. Brush with egg glaze. Bake in preheated oven at 400 degrees for 15 minutes, or until golden brown. Makes about 16 small turnovers.

Codfish Fritters

½ lb. salted codfish
½ cup all-purpose flour
1 heaping teaspoon baking powder
1 onion, minced
3 tablespoons water
2 tablespoons fresh parsley, chopped

2 eggs, well beaten
1 teaspoon salt
½ teaspoon pepper
1 clove garlic, minced
Vegetable oil or extra-virgin olive oil
  for frying

Cover codfish with water and soak overnight; change water 2 or 3 times. Fillet, removing dark skin. Shred meat finely with your hands and beat until light. Add flour, baking powder, and onion. Mix well and add water, parsley, eggs, salt, pepper, and garlic. Mix thoroughly.

Pour enough oil in skillet to deep-fry fritters. Drop mixture by teaspoonfuls into hot oil and fry until golden brown, turning once. Drain fritters on paper towel and serve hot. Makes about 18 fritters.

Empanadas
(Mexican Meat Pies)

2 cups boiled boneless pork roast (about 1 lb.)
1 bay leaf
2 cups boiled beef tongue (about 1 lb.)

1 cup currants
1 32-oz. jar mincemeat
½ cup pine nuts

In a pot with 4 cups of water, bring pork and bay leaf to a boil. Cover and cook 1 hour, until tender. In another pot, do the same with beef tongue. Let both pots cool. (*Note:* Tongue is sold only whole; slice what you need for the recipe.) Peel skin off tongue. Put both meats through a meat grinder or shred very fine with your hands.

In a large bowl, combine meat with currants, mincemeat, and pine nuts. Mix thoroughly.

Make pastry dough as in Pastry Dough recipe for Empanadas de Pollo (p. 21—double this recipe); you can also use ready-made dough, thawed and rolled out as in Pastry Dough recipe. Place 1 tablespoon of meat mixture in center of each 4-inch circle of dough. Moisten edges with water and fold over. Use a fork to crimp edges and prick top. Brush with egg glaze. Bake in a preheated oven at 400 degrees 15 minutes or until golden brown. Often served between meals at holiday time, with wine. Makes about 2 dozen meat pies.

VARIATION: PUMPKIN FILLING

1 cup pumpkin, fresh or canned	1 cup sugar
½ cup raisins	½ teaspoon powdered cloves
½ cup almonds, sliced	½ teaspoon allspice

If using fresh pumpkin, cook until tender and rub through a colander. Combine pumpkin with remaining ingredients. Halve the amount of dough used for the meat pies. Makes about 1 dozen pies.

Guacamole

4 or 5 avocados, peeled, cut up, and mashed	2 cloves garlic, minced
1 onion, diced	⅛ teaspoon red chili pepper
1 tomato, diced	
2 green chilies, roasted and chopped	Salt and pepper to taste
⅓ cup Taco Bell hot sauce	Garlic salt to taste

Mix avocados, onion, tomato, green chilies, hot sauce, and garlic. Add red chili, salt, pepper, and garlic salt to taste.

Salsa

1 large onion, chopped
3 jalapeño peppers, minced
¼ cup lemon juice
Salt and pepper to taste

2 fresh tomatoes, chopped
2 cloves garlic, minced
½ green bell pepper, chopped
¼ cup cilantro, chopped

Mix all ingredients except salt and pepper. Season to taste.

Chopped Liver

1 lb. poultry livers
3 tablespoons poultry fat
1 cup chopped onions

3 hard-boiled eggs
Salt and pepper to taste

Sauté livers in poultry fat until well done. Add onions. Put livers, onions, and eggs through a mincer. Season to taste. Serves 8–10.

Eggplant Caviar

1 small eggplant, unpeeled
1 onion
1 green bell pepper
1 4-oz. can mushrooms
1 clove garlic
⅓ cup extra-virgin olive oil
1 6-oz. can tomato paste

¼ cup water
2 tablespoons white wine vinegar
½ cup stuffed olives, chopped
3 tablespoons pine nuts, toasted
1½ teaspoons sugar
½ teaspoon oregano
Salt and pepper to taste

Finely chop the eggplant, onion, green pepper, mushrooms, and garlic. Place in a pot with the oil and simmer 10 minutes. Stir remaining ingredients into pot. Cover and simmer 30 minutes. Chill and serve cold. May be frozen. Makes about 2 cups.

The Incredible Nochebuena
Journey of Benito Juárez

My mother's side of the family, the Jimenez clan, migrated from La Coruña, Spain, to Mexico at the turn of the century. My grandfather Gustavo was in the diplomatic service and arrived in Veracruz with a wife and five children: three girls and two boys.

Gustavo Jimenez had a nose for business and soon he had expanded into the world of commerce, where he did very well. He bought a big house, staffed it with Indian servants, and had two more boys.

As in all big families, the children brought their own distinct personalities to bear on the family. Nevertheless, all were well-mannered, diligent in school, musically talented, and obedient to the strict, no-nonsense ways of their parents—all, that is, but one.

Paul was an exceedingly good-looking little boy with a Huck Finn disposition. Charm and a devilish sense of humor won him the love and adoration of the Indian servants, who would often shelter him from the harsh discipline of his parents.

The entire Jimenez family, 1910.

One of the earliest indications of Paul's mischievous nature came when he was about three. His world then consisted of a parrot named Alfonso (after the king of Spain), and Tatita, an Indian maid who loved the boy as if he were her own. In her efforts to potty-train the child, her custom was to sit him on the little toilet and then, because Paul liked to dawdle on the pot, return to her kitchen chores downstairs.

When he was ready, Paul would call down, "Ya acabe!" (I'm finished!). He would repeat the phrase with growing urgency as his patience wore thin, until finally the accent was on the last syllable: "Ya acabee-ee-ee-ee-ee-ee!" At last, Tatita would drop what she was doing and run to attend to Paul's needs.

Before long, Paul had taught Alfonso the parrot to mimic him perfectly. "Ya acabee-ee-ee-ee" Alfonso would screech, causing poor Tatita many futile trips up the stairs only to find the boy laughing with delight.

One day, to no one's astonishment, the parrot Alfonso disappeared. Don Gustavo surmised correctly that Tatita had taken the bird home to her family; nor did he disapprove.

"How was she?" asked Don Gustavo.

"Very good with mustard," answered Tatita, her face as hard and straight as the faces on the Olmec statues.

When Paul grew old enough to attend school, Don Gustavo decided to send him to a public school rather than hire private tutors. Whereas his other six children had exhibited high intelligence and a readiness to learn, Paul demonstrated no such abilities. He was an indifferent learner with no particular curiosity about anything other than that which immediately surrounded him. While his siblings adopted the autocratic airs of the rich and privileged and even a certain arrogance about being native-born Spaniards, Paul immediately fell in with the lower classes, native-born Mexicans, and, to the horror of his family, Indian boys.

"Paul has a broad affinity for vulgarity," Don Gustavo observed.

Soon Paul was skipping school and hanging out with the "rough" boys on the docks. Repeatedly confronted with complaints about his son from teachers and policemen, Don Gustavo lost his patience. Beatings had not been a deterrent, nor had a diet of bread and water dampened Paul's devilishness, so Don Gustavo resorted to the worst punishment he knew. He took Paul down to the basement one Saturday and hung him up by his thumbs. Here Paul was to remain for the weekend, being let down only to eat some bread and water and to sleep. The family was horrified, but all agreed that something drastic had to be done before Paul ruined his life.

Paul was at this time a young man of about twelve. A stunningly handsome boy, his charming way with the opposite sex was already apparent. This may have had something to do with the Indian maids' response to Paul's harsh punishment. No sooner had Paul been hung up by his thumbs and his sorrowful family returned to the upstairs living quarters, than the maids were busy untying Paul and bringing him plates of chicken fajitas and chili.

Paul's father was naturally bewildered by his son's extraordinary stoicism. A weekend of being hung by his thumbs in the cellar and restricted to a diet of bread and water seemed not to bother Paul. In fact, if anything, he had gained weight over the long weekend. Don Gustavo threw up his hands and gave up.

One day, however, the problem of disciplining Paul was solved in an unexpected way. Paul had found a scruffy puppy on the docks, abandoned by a freighter of Polish sailors. Paul took the dog home and thereafter devoted every minute to caring for the sickly puppy. Paul's sole obsession, the dog provided Don Gustavo with an effective "or else." From that point on, every paternal order was obeyed—"or else" the dog would be thrown out. For the first time in his life Paul became a model son. His attendance at school was perfect, his conduct impeccable, and even his grades rose dramatically, to the genuine astonishment of his parents and teachers.

The puppy grew to be a huge dog, the product of a gene pool that included German shepherd, a bit of chow, and a great deal of wolf. Named Benito Juárez (after the Mexican Liberator), he was an excellent watchdog and correctly sensed whom to bite and whom to protect. Kind and gentle with the children and the Indian maids, he seemed to have a distrust of Paul's father and mother and would leave the room whenever they entered, never allowing them to pet him.

A year passed without incident, after which Don Gustavo entered into a business transaction that necessitated moving his family to Monterrey, in Mexico's northern interior. Everyone in the family was happy about the move—everyone, that is, but Paul, who looked upon it as a curse, for he would be deprived of the company of his Indian pals, his friends on the docks, and the lovely afternoons spent watching the sailing vessels come and go.

Once in Monterrey, Paul reverted to his early character, skipping school and seeking the company of local street urchins. His dog followed suit and began biting everyone and anyone indiscriminately. Angry complaints began to pour in to Don Gustavo. Benito Juárez had bitten every delivery man, mailman, gardener, and guest to appear at the door. The end came when he spied Paul's mother, my grandmother, who had forgotten her key, crawling in through the kitchen window. Mistaking her for a burglar, he bit her hard on the buttock.

It was secretly decided that Don Gustavo would take Benito Juárez with him on the train to Mexico City, where he had business to do. He would abandon the dog in the middle of the city, and that would be that.

But how to tell Paul? Don Gustavo and his wife decided to lie and stonewall it. No one in the family, not even the Indian maids, were told of the plan. Don Gustavo agonized about the effect Benito's disappearance would have on Paul, but decided that the dog-wolf must go. It was hard, but it was for the best. When the time came, he had the dog drugged and put in his compartment on the train to Mexico City.

Predictably, Paul went into a deep depression. He searched all of Monterrey, but no one had seen his dog. He checked continuously at the dog pound, but no Benito Juárez. Paul's attendance in school plummeted. His grades followed suit. Don Gustavo began to doubt his decision, but now the damage was done—Benito Juárez was history.

The Christmas holidays were upon them, and the entire family entered into the spirit of merriment and grand expectation that precedes the huge feast of Nochebuena. The year had been bountiful for the family, and the guest list for Nochebuena grew and grew.

Only Paul remained uncharacteristically sullen and depressed. He missed Benito Juárez, his best friend and protector. Four months had passed since the dog's mysterious disappearance, and still Paul went looking every day, far into the countryside, for his dog. No one, not even his favorite maid, had a clue about Benito's mysterious disappearance. The dog had simply vanished.

At last it was Nochebuena time. The table was loaded with blackened chicken, fajitas, tortillas, red beans, mole, chili, a large roasted pig, and every kind of fruit and vegetable in Mexico.

It was the custom of the Jimenez family, seated around the Nochebuena table, to have each child get up and name the one gift they would like to have above all others. So one by one, each of the children stood and recited his or her deepest desire—each one, that is, except Paul. When his turn came, Paul refused to get up.

Seated around the table, the guests laughed nervously and looked at Don Gustavo, who looked apoplectic. His face red, his huge moustache bristling, he gave Paul a hard stare. At long last, his father's glare served to draw Paul slowly up from his chair. He stood in his fine white linen suit, his handsome head hung low. He remained silent.

"Well, what is it you wish for?!" Don Gustavo exploded, causing his guests to look down at their plates in embarrassment.

"Benito Juárez," Paul said in a low voice.

"Benito Juárez? Why, he died years ago," said one of the guests, an old retired general.

"No, no—not Benito the Liberator. The child had a dog named Benito Juárez who disappeared last August," said his wife.

"Oh, that," said the general, returning to his chili.

No one who was there that night remembers the precise hour at which the loud commotion in front of the house began. The noise grew louder and louder until it seemed as if the huge old door would give way.

The butler hastened to the door, when, much to everyone's surprise, in bounded Benito Juárez! Dust-covered and ragged, the dog ran straight into the arms of the delighted Paul.

Great was the merriment in the big hall that happy night. Even Don Gustavo and my grandmother, who had long since admitted to themselves their terrible error, were overwhelmed with joy.

And so it was, according to my Uncle Paul—the family storyteller and wit—that the Jimenez family's best Nochebuena ever was celebrated in Monterrey, Mexico—before Porfirio Díaz was brought down by Villa, Carranza, and Zapata; before the Revolution of 1910; and before the family was driven out of Mexico in flatcars to seek a new life in a place called the United States.

Had the Indian maids not sewn up the family gold, silver, and jewels into the girls' petticoats, the Jimenez family would have landed in Galveston destitute, with only one treasure to their name: a fierce watchdog named Benito Juárez.

My uncle Paul Jimenez lived a simple, modest life, but a long one. Wherever he went he was always welcome, for he had a way with a story—and if, in the story's telling, the truth was bent or circumvented a little bit, no one ever minded. But as for the story of Benito Juárez's incredible journey from Mexico City to Monterrey—a distance of 450 miles over a four-month period—Uncle Paul swore to the end of his life that it was true to its last detail, and no one in the family ever denied it.

Every Nochebuena while Don Gustavo lived, someone would cry out, "Tell the story of Benito Juárez and the long trip!" And Uncle Paul would stand up and tell his story. Every year it got longer—sometimes funnier, sometimes sadder—but always the end was the same, and always, everyone cried.

Mr. Ybor's First Nochebuena

Vicente Martinez Ybor sat at his desk, in his office, inside his new cigar factory on 14th Street between 8th and 9th Avenues. It was in Ybor City, the immigrant community that had grown up around the cigar factories of Tampa, Florida, and was named for himself. It was December, 1886. Ybor had moved his business from Key West to the Tampa area, bringing with him his Cuban and Spanish immigrant *tabaqueros* (cigar makers). The factory was already a success, famous for the high quality and wonderful aroma of its hand-rolled El Principe De Galles (Prince of Wales) cigars.

Ybor's every business decision had seemed charmed, but now he faced a crisis. Living conditions for the workers were abominable. Streets and sidewalks were few, palmetto scrubs were many. The small clapboard, tin-roofed houses in which the workers lived were ovens in the summer and refrigerators in the winter. Rattlesnake nests and alligator holes made even a trip to the "two-holer" outhouse a perilous adventure. In the factory, swarms of mosquitoes, gnats, and mites often made it necessary for the *tabaqueros* to wear goggles in order to keep the insects out of their eyes. The workers were openly dissatisfied and rebellious.

La Quinta, the home of Vicente M. Ybor.

With the Christmas holiday fast approaching, Ybor knew he had no time to spare. His workers would leave to spend their holidays with family and friends in Key West and Havana, and they would never return. Once back in their comfortable homes, warm with the glow of Nochebuena, they would not for a moment think of returning to the primitive, rough-and-ready life waiting for them in Ybor City. He had to find a way to head off this mass desertion. He had to give his workers a reason to call Ybor City home.

Together with his wife, Ybor City's first visionary came up with a plan that was simplicity itself. For Nochebuena, he would invite each of the workers and their families to his home, La Quinta, a large, two-story mansion on 12th Avenue and 16th Street that was the envy of all, though few workers had ever been inside the big house. Ybor promised a lavish feast, and a surprise—one that no one would ever forget.

Sure enough, every last worker accepted the offer and chose to stay in Ybor that Christmas Eve, and each had his own idea about what the surprise would be. At the factory, in the days leading up to Christmas Eve, the workers buzzed with anticipation and excitement. At last, it was Nochebuena. The guests arrived in droves. Dozens of tables were set out on the lawn. Japanese lanterns swung in the breeze, and candles flickered on the tables. In the surrounding grove of orange trees, small candles glowed in the tree branches. It was a magical sight.

The wine flowed, and servants carried out platters of *lechón asado* (roast pig), turkey, red snapper, chickens—and then they carried out *more* platters, heaped this time with mounds of succulent yellow rice, black beans, *yucca,* roasted potatoes, and every vegetable imaginable. On a dessert table were *turrones,* soft and hard, walnuts, pecans, figs, grapes, watermelons, cantaloupes, and a mouth-watering variety of bakery masterpieces. Everyone agreed it was the best meal they had eaten since they had arrived in the wilderness. *Cafés solos* were served, the men lit up their *puros* (cigars), and everyone sat back to wait for Ybor's surprise.

Ybor stood behind a table, a big box in front of him. The crowd came to a respectful silence, and he began: "Workers of the Ybor City Cigar Factory! For one year you have worked long and hard under trying conditions for your families! Tonight on Christmas Eve, I want to announce my gift to you." He paused for effect.

"In this box I have the entire profits we have made this year. I have divided it equally among each worker. Each person working at my factory gets one equal share. Let us enjoy Nochebuena and the holidays together as a family, and pray for another prosperous New Year."

Nor was this any small boast, as the workers well knew. The profits that year amounted to $6,000—a fine sum, in 1886. Each worker would receive what amounted to three or four weeks' worth of wages.

After a moment of shocked disbelief, the assembled workers broke into a spontaneous cheer, then lined up to receive their shares of the Ybor Cigar Factory profits.

In the hundred-year history of Ybor City, such a Nochebuena never happened again, but in fact, it was a miracle that it ever happened at all. In years to come, Ybor would build better housing for his workers and the scrub wilderness would be transformed into a thriving and vibrant community—but none of it would have happened had Vicente Ybor not won the loyalty and love of his workers that first Nochebuena in Ybor City, long ago.

Soups and Stews

Turkey Stock Soup

2 cups turkey stock
1 onion, chopped
½ cup green beans, sliced
1 cup blackeye peas, cooked

1 cup rice, cooked
½ cup corn
Salt and pepper to taste

To make turkey stock, follow recipe for Chicken Broth below, substituting turkey. Add onions to stock; simmer for 20 minutes. Add other ingredients except salt and pepper, and simmer for ½ hour. Season to taste. Serves 6.

Chicken Broth

1 3½ to 4 lb. chicken and giblets
  (not liver)
4 medium onions, peeled and quartered
1 carrot, scraped and cut in pieces
6 garlic cloves, crushed

1 2-inch strip green bell
  pepper
5 quarts water
Salt to taste
¼ teaspoon saffron or yellow
  food coloring

Place chicken and giblets (whole or cut up) in a large stockpot. Add 5 quarts of water. When it comes to a boil, remove foam with a skimmer. Add rest of ingredients. Cover and boil 1½ hours. Remove from stove; strain. Refrigerate clear broth until fat rises and gels solidify. Skim fat from top. Remove chicken from bones and use separately.

Chestnut Soup

1 lb. raw chestnuts
1 cup water
1 onion, finely chopped
1½ tablespoons butter
½ tablespoon extra-virgin olive oil
4 cups chicken broth (homemade
  preferred, but canned may be substituted)

⅛ teaspoon powdered mace
⅛ teaspoon cayenne pepper
Salt and pepper to taste
2 cups light cream
Fresh parsley, for garnish
Croutons, for garnish

Preheat oven to 400 degrees. Using a sharp knife, slit the shiny brown skin of each chestnut into a cross. Arrange chestnuts in a single layer, flat side down, on a roasting tray. Pour 1 cup water into the tray. Roast chestnuts in oven for about 8 minutes and peel while they are still hot. Sauté chopped onion with butter and oil.

Put peeled chestnuts into a large pot and cover with broth and sautéed onions. Bring to a boil, skim, cover, and simmer for 45 minutes, or until chestnuts are easily broken by pressing them with a wooden spoon. Strain and reserve broth. Purée chestnuts in a blender with a small amount of broth.

Rinse pot and return chestnuts to it. Gradually stir in broth and season with mace, cayenne, sugar, salt, and pepper. Bring soup to a boil; reduce heat. Just before serving, stir in cream. Serve the soup very hot, but do not boil it again once cream has been added. Add salt and pepper to taste. Garnish with parsley and croutons. Serves 4.

Note: The flavor and sweetness of fresh chestnuts can vary. If the chestnuts are very sweet, the soup may be too sweet for some tastes. This can be modified by eliminating the sugar or by stewing the chestnuts in water rather than broth and adding fresh broth to the purée instead.

Spaghettini in Broth

1 cup thin spaghetti
   broken in 1½-inch pieces
8 cups chicken broth (see p. 38)

1 quart water
2 eggs, well beaten
⅓ cup Romano cheese, grated

Cook spaghettini *al dente* in salted water (about 8 minutes) and drain. Bring chicken broth to boil; add spaghettini. Remove from heat and add eggs, stirring rapidly until the eggs float in strings. Serve sprinkled with cheese. Serves 6.

Home-Style Minestrone

½ cup navy beans
1 tablespoon extra-virgin olive oil
2 onions, chopped
2 cloves garlic, crushed
4 tomatoes, chopped
8 cups water
1 teaspoon fresh marjoram, chopped,
   or 1 teaspoon dry marjoram
1 teaspoon fresh thyme, chopped,
   or 1 teaspoon dry thyme
2 carrots, diced

2 potatoes, diced
1 small turnip, diced
2 stalks celery, finely sliced
3 cups grated cabbage
½ cup macaroni pieces or
   small pasta shells, stars, etc.
1 tablespoon fresh parsley,
   chopped
Salt and pepper to taste
Grated Parmesan cheese

Soak beans overnight in cold water to cover. Heat oil in a large pot, add onions and garlic, and sauté briefly. Add tomatoes, beans, water, marjoram, and thyme and simmer covered for about 2 hours. Add carrots, cook for about 15 minutes, then add potatoes and turnip. Cook for 5 more minutes and add celery, cabbage, and pasta.

    Continue cooking until pasta and all the vegetables are tender, about 10–15 minutes. Add parsley, then salt and pepper to taste. Serve sprinkled with Parmesan cheese. Serves 8.

Burrida
(Genoese Fish Stew)

4 lbs. fish, filleted
¾ cup extra-virgin olive oil
2 cloves garlic, crushed
1 large mild onion, finely chopped
2 anchovy fillets, minced
1 16-oz. can peeled tomatoes,
  sliced (including juice)
½ cup fresh parsley, chopped

2 cups dry white wine
1 bay leaf
¼ teaspoon crushed fennel seed
¼ teaspoon crushed saffron
1 teaspoon salt
¼ teaspoon pepper
6 slices Italian bread, toasted

Use any kind of fish fillets; whitefish, red snapper, haddock, mackerel, and rock salmon are good choices. Remove skin and cut fillets into 2⅓–3 inch pieces. Heat oil in a heavy pot over medium heat. Add garlic; do not let it brown. Add onions; cook until just tender. Add anchovies, parsley, wine, and tomatoes, undrained.

Cook for 10 minutes over low heat. Add fish, bay leaf, fennel seed, saffron, and salt and pepper to taste. Simmer for an additional 20 minutes. Serve with bread slices on top. Serves 6.

Escudella
(Peasant Soup)

½ cup dried chickpeas
½ cup dried white beans
1 lb. bacon or ham hock
6 ozs. salt pork, cut in cubes
1 bay leaf
1 small onion, whole
9 cups water
4 ozs. blood sausage, sliced
6 ozs. sausage, sliced

2 large potatoes, peeled and cubed
2 medium carrots, peeled and diced
1 medium turnip, peeled and diced
1 cup chopped turnip/beet greens
1 large onion, chopped
¼ cup short-grain rice
½ cup egg noodles, broken in pieces
1½ teaspoons salt
½ teaspoon pepper

Soak chickpeas and white beans in bowl of water overnight; then drain. In a large pot cover chickpeas with water and bring to a boil; reduce heat and simmer for 2 hours, skimming occasionally. Drain. In the same pot add drained white beans, bacon or ham hock, salt pork, bay leaf, and onion. Add 9 cups water and bring to a boil; reduce heat and simmer for 2½ hours.

Remove onion and bacon or ham hock. Scrape meat from bone, discard bone and skin, and cut meat into small cubes; set aside. Add remaining ingredients (and more water to cover if necessary). Simmer for about 20 minutes; add cubed meat and simmer 10 minutes longer. Correct seasoning. Usually served on Christmas Day in the northern part of Spain. Serves 6.

Almond Soup

1⅓ cups blanched almonds
4 cloves garlic
4 tablespoons extra-virgin olive oil
½ teaspoon salt

10 cups water
4 teaspoons white wine vinegar
Cinnamon, 24 seedless white grapes
  (peeled), or rose petals, for garnish

Crush almonds, garlic, olive oil, and salt to a smooth paste, using an electric blender. Gradually add 10 cups water. Correct seasoning. Chill. Just before serving, stir in vinegar. Serve in individual bowls with a garnish of grapes or a sprinkling of cinnamon, or float a single rose petal in each bowl. Serves 8.

Spanish Bean Soup

½ lb. garbanzo beans (chickpeas)
1 tablespoon salt
2 quarts water
1 ham bone
1 beef bone
¼ lb. salt pork

1 onion, finely chopped
2 potatoes, quartered
⅛ teaspoon saffron
½ teaspoon paprika
Salt to taste
1 *chorizo* (Spanish sausage), thinly
  sliced

Wash garbanzos. Soak overnight with 1 tablespoon salt, in water to cover. When ready to cook, drain beans. Place in 4-quart soup kettle, add 2 quarts of water, ham bone, and beef bone. Cook for 45 minutes over low heat, occasionally skimming off foam. Cut salt pork in thin strips and fry slowly in a skillet. Add chopped onion, sauté briefly, and add to beans along with potatoes, paprika, and saffron. Salt to taste. When potatoes are done, remove from heat. Add *chorizo*. Serves 4.

Menudo

2 lbs. tripe, diced
3 quarts water
2 pig's feet
2 country pork ribs, or 2 ham hocks
2 cloves garlic, crushed

1 onion, finely chopped
1 bay leaf
1 28-oz. can hominy, undrained
3 tablespoons chili powder
Garnishes: chopped onions,
  oregano, dried red chili peppers

Rinse tripe in clear water and chop into small squares. Bring about 3 quarts of water to a boil; add tripe, pig's feet, pork ribs or ham hocks, onion, garlic, and bay leaf. Reduce heat and simmer for 3 hours. Add hominy and chili sauce or powder. Simmer 1 more hour. Season to taste. Garnish with onions, oregano, and dried red chili peppers.

Mexican Chili Soup

3 chicken breasts
3 cups chicken broth, homemade
  (see p. 38) or canned
2 tablespoons cornmeal
⅛ teaspoon cumin powder

3 tablespoons red chili powder
2 large garlic cloves, chopped
6 corn tortillas, cut in strips
2 tablespoons vegetable oil

Boil chicken in broth until tender; add salt to taste. Remove chicken and set aside to cool. Mix cornmeal, cumin powder, chili powder, and garlic; add to broth and stir. Bring mixture to a boil, lower heat, and simmer for 10 minutes or until mixture thickens.

Cut or shred chicken and add to mixture, which should be as thick as gravy. Simmer for another 10 minutes. Fry tortilla strips in oil, drain, place in bottom of soup bowls, and ladle soup over them. Serves 4.

Corn Soup

3½ cups fresh or frozen corn kernels
1 cup chicken broth, homemade
  (see p. 38) or canned
4 tablespoons butter
2 cups milk
1 teaspoon cumin
1 clove garlic, minced
1 4-oz. can green chili peppers
1 teaspoon Tabasco sauce
1 teaspoon white pepper
8 corn tortillas

½ cup vegetable oil
1 cup fresh tomatoes, diced
2 cups diced cooked chicken breasts
1 cup Monterey Jack cheese with
  jalapeño peppers, shredded
Condiments:
1 cup chunky salsa
1 cup black olives, sliced
1 cup sour cream
½ cup scallions, sliced
1 cup avocado, diced

In a blender or food processor, purée corn and chicken broth. Melt butter in stockpot. Add purée and simmer over low heat for 5 minutes, stirring constantly. Stir in milk, cumin, and garlic. Heat to boiling, reduce heat, and stir in green chilies, Tabasco sauce, and white pepper.

    Stack tortillas and cut into 1-inch squares. Heat ½ inch of oil in a heavy skillet and fry tortilla squares until golden (only a few seconds, as they brown very fast). Drain on paper towels and sprinkle with salt. Place equal amounts of diced tomatoes and chicken in individual bowls. Add shredded cheese to simmering soup and stir until cheese melts. Ladle soup into bowls and garnish with tortilla squares. Serve condiments to be added as desired. Serves 6–8.

Mushroom Barley Soup

2 tablespoons navy beans
1 cup barley
1 large soup bone
1 lb. brisket of beef
3 quarts water
2 celery stalks, finely diced

2 carrots, diced
2 onions, diced
10 dried imported mushrooms, or
  ½ lb. fresh mushrooms, sliced
1 tablespoon salt
1 bay leaf
¼ teaspoon pepper

Rinse beans and barley. In large pot cook beans, barley, soup bone, and beef in water for 1 hour, beginning with medium heat and lowering to simmer after 15 minutes. Skim surface. Add remaining ingredients and simmer for another hour. Serves 8.

Chicken Soup with Kreplach

SOUP

1 boiling chicken
2 quarts water
3 carrots, scraped
3 onions
2 potatoes, quartered

2 parsnips, halved
1 summer squash, halved
3 stalks celery, with leaves
2 teaspoons salt
¼ teaspoon pepper

Cut up chicken in quarters, season with salt and pepper, and boil with remaining ingredients. Cook over low heat for 1 hour, or until the chicken is very tender and the vegetables done. Strain; reserve broth.

NOODLE DOUGH

2 eggs
½ teaspoon salt

2 cups sifted all-purpose flour

Kreplach are triangular or square pastalike pockets with various fillings. To make the dough, beat eggs and salt slightly. Add flour; use more, if needed, to make a stiff dough. Knead well, until dough is soft and elastic. Roll out very thin. Do not allow to dry out. Cut into 2-inch squares. Place 1 tablespoon of filling (see below) on each square. Fold crosswise into a triangle, pressing edges together. Drop triangles into simmering chicken broth (see above) and cook for 15 more minutes. Serves 8.

FILLING FOR KREPLACH

1 teaspoon chopped onion
1 egg
2–3 cups chicken (cooked in
 soup recipe above), chopped

1 tablespoon fresh parsley, chopped
1 teaspoon salt
¼ teaspoon pepper

Mix all ingredients well.

Sephardic Garlic Soup

3 tablespoons vegetable oil
¾ cup stale bread, thinly sliced
4 cloves garlic
¼ teaspoon paprika

4½ cups water
1 teaspoon salt
2 tablespoons milk

Heat oil in a large skillet until golden brown. Add bread and garlic, and fry. Leaving oil in skillet, put bread and garlic into an ovenproof tureen. Stir paprika thoroughly into oil. Remove skillet from heat.

 In a small pot, add salt to water and bring to a boil. Pour over bread and garlic in tureen, cover, and let stand 5 minutes. Remove garlic and discard. Add milk to oil in skillet, mix, pour into soup tureen, and stir well. Place in 350-degree oven for 5–6 minutes, until bread floats to the surface and has a nice, crusty brown top. Serves 6.

Meatless Vegetable Soup

1 large onion, chopped
4 tablespoons butter, melted
½ cup carrots, diced
⅓ cup cabbage, shredded
½ cup green peas
¼ cup celery, diced
¼ cup green beans, sliced

1½ cups potatoes, diced
6 cups water
1 cup canned tomatoes
2 teaspoons fresh parsley, chopped
1 parsnip, diced
1 teaspoon sugar
1 teaspoon salt

In a large pot, sauté onion in melted butter until translucent. Add remaining vegetables, except potatoes and tomatoes, and cook 10 minutes, stirring constantly. Add potatoes, water, seasoning, and tomatoes. Simmer until vegetables are tender. Serves 6–8.

Split Pea Soup

1 lb. green or yellow split peas
3 quarts homemade chicken broth (see
    p. 38), or 1 50-oz. can chicken broth
3 carrots, shredded
2 medium white onions, finely chopped
⅛ teaspoon white pepper

Garnishes (optional):
1 cup garlic croutons
1 cup sour cream
2 kosher hot dogs, cooked and
    sliced

Wash and drain peas. In a large pot place peas, broth, and rest of ingredients, except pepper. Bring broth to a boil, lower heat, and simmer for 2 hours. Add pepper. Purée in a blender or food processor at low speed. Garnish if desired. Serves 8.

Old Man Cuscaden's
Nochebuena Gift

Major Augustine Fernandez, USAF, retired, sat quietly in a Spanish restaurant, the Madrid, contemplating his steaming plate of *cocido* (Spanish stew). I had asked him what he remembered most about Nochebuena and if anything unusual had ever happened on that day. After thinking a long while, he said simply, "Nochebuena was the worst day of the year."

I was shocked. "Why? Didn't you get enough to eat?"

"Sure," he said, "but every Nochebuena my father made me go with him out to the pigpen and hold the pig while he butchered it. The pig's screams were so dreadful that I had nightmares for months afterwards."

But Augustine Fernandez did have a good Nochebuena memory to tell me about.

In Ybor City in the late 1920s and '30s, Augustine Fernandez was known as Chunchi. He was sweet and good-natured but would fight at the drop of a hat—and what was more, he packed a knock-out punch. Chunchi never backed down to anyone and seemed generally immune to fear.

Chunchi's parents had come from Spain; his father was from Salas, his mother from Santander, so they were considered Asturianos. The Fernandez family farm was situated at the edge of a great orange and grapefruit grove which belonged to a pioneer family named Cuscaden, who in 1848 had built the first house in that part of the country. It was a small cracker house with a porch and tin roof.

The sour old cracker who owned and ran the orange grove was the terror of the neighborhood kids. His name was Arthur Cuscaden. His favorite pastime was to sit on his porch with a double-barreled shotgun in his lap. He loaded it with salt, not buckshot, and it seemed to give him great pleasure to shoot trespassers, whether they were stealing his oranges or not. A backside full of salt was a mighty deterrent to the kids of Chunchi's neighborhood—but not to Chunchi.

Chunchi had three reasons for not being able to stay off old Cuscaden's property. The first was that he always traveled to school with a pocketful of smooth rocks. These rocks were part of the fill that a contractor had dumped at a corner of Cuscaden's property. Chunchi had a major-league arm and could pretty well hit any target he aimed for with stinging force. This kept the gang kids at bay. Both gangs at V. M. Ybor Elementary School had tried to recruit him, but Chunchi was a lone eagle and refused to join either of them.

The second reason Chunchi had to trespass on Cuscaden's property was to get to the water tower located near Cuscaden's grove, so that he could throw rocks at it. To Chunchi, the clanging of the rocks against the tower was a lovely noise.

But Chunchi's biggest problem was that he had to take care of his family's milk cow every morning, which meant he was always in a hurry. If he couldn't cut through Cuscaden's property, he would be late to school and so get punished. To make matters worse, at lunchtime he had to repeat the journey so that he could untie the cow and move it out of the sun and tie it up under a tree for shade. Again, the trip was too long to make it in time without going through Cuscaden's property, so the only course open

Gus "Chunchi" Fernandez as a child.

to little Chunchi was to race diagonally through the grove as fast as his legs would take him, hoping against hope that Cuscaden was sleeping off the previous night's drunk, or that his nocturnal vigil, watching for interlopers, had kept him awake until dawn.

Old Cuscaden observed little Chunchi's fear-propelled flights with interest, but it was some time before he decided to act.

One day, as Chunchi was doing his road-runner flight through Cuscaden's grove, he heard a whistle. It was low and insistent and sounded like no whistle Chunchi had ever heard before, but he knew it was Cuscaden calling him to the porch. He froze, the image of Cuscaden's twelve-gauge, salt-filled shotgun etched in his mind.

Cuscaden was sitting in his chair, the shotgun in his lap. Chunchi sidled up to the porch, his hand on one of the bigger rocks in his pocket. If he had to go down, at least he would bounce one off the old man's noggin.

The old man motioned to a burlap bag filled with oranges that lay next

Chunchi Runs the Blockade.

to his chair. It was almost Christmastime, and Nochebuena was just around the corner. He motioned again for Chunchi to take it. So he was sending Chunchi home with fruit for his parent's Nochebuena table! Chunchi couldn't believe it.

Then, in his rough old man's voice, Cuscaden said, "Boy, you don't have to run so darned fast through my orchard. From now on, you can cross it as many times a day as you want."

So Chunchi grew up running through the old man's grove without getting shot at, sometimes leaving a plate of his mother's famous candied yams on the porch for the old cracker. And when his family fed their cow with vines from the sweet potato plant, making it produce a thick, creamy, sweet milk, Chunchi would leave some in a pail by the door for Old Man Cuscaden.

But Cuscaden never spoke to Chunchi again during all the years Chunchi went to V. M. Ybor Elementary School. From time to time the old man would whistle his low, insistent, birdlike call, and Chunchi would go running to receive his bag of oranges, grapefruits, or pecans, but Cuscaden always slipped back into his house before Chunchi could say anything— which was just as well, since he could never think of anything to say to Mr. Cuscaden anyhow.

One night years later, Mr. Cuscaden came home late and inebriated only to find his front door locked. Not wanting to awaken his wife, with whom he was having violent quarrels, he decided to enter the house through an unlocked porch window. Very much to his surprise, he found his agitated wife waiting inside, the twelve-gauge shotgun in her hands and pointed at *him*. And that was the last thing Mr. Cuscaden saw before he left this life.

This was a big scandal for the Ybor City community, but Cuscaden still had one surprise left of his own. The City of Tampa had already taken half his land in order to settle the matter of some back taxes. In his will, however, Cuscaden left the rest of the land to the city with the provision that they build a park on it for the kids of Ybor City. Thus, Cuscaden Park was built, much of it by the W.P.A. workforce, and it quickly became the focal point of all recreation and sports in Ybor City.

Chunchi grew into a tough young man, going straight from Hillsborough High to air cadet school to the Eighth Air Corps in England. It was 1942. His next Nochebuena whistle was the sergeant's wake-up whistle that had him crawling into the nose of a B-17 to deliver bombs down German chimneys. And the lovely noise of his flat rocks hitting the water tower was replaced by the frightful noise of flak hitting the metal fuselage of his B-17 bomber. Chunchi's Nochebuena in Europe ended finally in a prisoner-of-

Captain Gus "Chunchi" Fernandez as a bombardier in the U.S. Army Air Force.

war camp on the frigid shores of the Baltic Sea, where for two years the best that Chunchi could hope for on Nochebuena was an extra bowl of cabbage soup.

Chunchi survived the war, received a college education at Florida State University, married a wonderful woman named Dorothy, rose to the rank of major in the United States Air Force, and now lives in Miami, a long way from Cuscaden Park. Every year at Nochebuena he remembers his strange relationship with the mean old man who owned the grove, and their unexpected friendship.

And back in Ybor City, Cuscaden Park still stands as a reminder of the special place an old man had in his heart for a tough little Spanish kid who could bounce flat rocks off a water tower, run fast, fight hard, and who always came running when the old man whistled.

Salads

Caesar Salad

Prepare salad of romaine lettuce, unseasoned croutons, and shaved, fresh Parmesan cheese. Toss with the following dressing. Add pepper to taste.

1 2-oz. can flat anchovies
¼ cup lemon juice, freshly squeezed
3 cloves garlic
½ teaspoon dry mustard
½ teaspoon sugar

1 cup extra-virgin olive oil
½ cup grated Parmesan cheese
1 egg
¾ teaspoon Worcestershire sauce

Put all ingredients in food processor or blender. Purée until smooth. Refrigerate 1 hour. Makes 1½ cups.

Olive Salad

1–1½ lbs. green olives, pitted
1½ lbs. black olives, pitted
4 1½-oz. boxes raisins
2 large white or red onions, sliced
4 stalks celery, sliced

4 3¼-oz. jars capers, rinsed and drained
2 tablespoons sugar
1 teaspoon oregano
2 cups extra-virgin olive oil
1 cup red wine vinegar

Soak olives in enough water to cover, 10–15 minutes. Drain and put in large container. Add raisins, onions, celery, capers, and sugar. Mix well. Sprinkle with oregano. Add oil and vinegar. Mix well and refrigerate in an airtight container overnight. Makes 4 cups.

Tomato Salad with Basil

1 large head romaine lettuce
10 ripe tomatoes, thickly sliced
16 ozs. mozzarella cheese,
   sliced ¼ inch thick
2 large red onions, peeled and sliced
½ cup extra-virgin olive oil
¼ cup white wine vinegar

½ cup pine nuts
5 cloves garlic
2 cups fresh basil leaves, or 3
   tablespoons dry basil
1 bunch parsley, stems removed
½ cup Parmesan cheese, grated
Salt and pepper to taste

On a round serving dish, place washed lettuce leaves and overlapping slices of tomato, mozzarella, and onion. Add dressing just before serving.

    To make the dressing, combine garlic, basil, parsley, cheese, oil, and pine nuts. Blend in a food processor or blender until smooth. Mix well with vinegar. Add salt and pepper to taste. Serves 4–6.

Shellfish Vinaigrette

1 quart water
1 cup clam broth
2 sprigs fresh rosemary
1 bay leaf
1 slice lemon
4 sprigs parsley

2 slices onion
2 cloves garlic, crushed
6 peppercorns
1 lb. large shrimps, unpeeled
1 lobster, with shell
1 lb. cooked crabmeat (blue crab,
   king crab, or stone crab)

In a large pot simmer first 9 ingredients for 20 minutes. Add lobster; boil for 15 minutes. Remove from liquid and cool. Add shrimp; boil for 4 minutes. Remove from liquid and cool. Shell shrimp and lobster. Cut lobster into chunks. Set aside to cool; make following sauce.

1 cup extra-virgin olive oil
1 cup white wine vinegar
¼ cup minced Spanish sweet onions
¼ cup capers

Mix all ingredients in a china or glass bowl. Add shrimp, lobster, and crabmeat. Mix well and chill overnight. Add salt and pepper to taste. Serves 4.

Watercress and Tomato Salad

2 heads romaine lettuce, roughly chopped
2 bunches watercress (stems removed), chopped
2 green tomatoes, quartered
1 bunch radishes, sliced
2 red tomatoes, quartered
2 cucumbers, peeled and sliced

In a salad bowl combine romaine, watercress, tomatoes, cucumbers, and radishes. Toss with Garlic Salad Dressing. Serves 6.

Garlic Salad Dressing

½ cup white vinegar
1½ cups extra-virgin olive oil
2 teaspoons salt
¼ teaspoon pepper
1 teaspoon powdered mustard
4 garlic cloves, finely minced
1 teaspoon oregano

Mix all ingredients well with wire whisk. Serve at room temperature. Makes 2 cups.

Parsley, Mint, and Watercress Salad

1 large bunch Italian parsley
  (stems removed), chopped
1 large bunch fresh mint, chopped
2 bunches watercress
  (stems removed), chopped

6 cloves garlic, thinly sliced
¾ cup extra-virgin olive oil
3 tablespoons fresh lemon juice
Salt and pepper to taste

Combine parsley, mint, and watercress in large salad bowl. Blend garlic, olive oil, and lemon juice in a blender and pour over salad. Toss salad, add salt and pepper. Serves 4–6.

Cauliflower Salad

1 large cauliflower
2 cloves garlic, finely chopped
18 black olives, pitted
1 tablespoon capers
¼ cup extra-virgin olive oil

1 tablespoon lemon juice
1 teaspoon superfine granulated sugar
1 teaspoon dry mustard
½ teaspoon salt
Pepper, freshly ground, to taste

Cut off green leaves and tough central stalk of cauliflower and break the head into florets. Cook cauliflower in a large pot of boiling salted water until it is just tender, but still slightly crisp; drain and cool. Rub serving bowl or dish with a cut clove of garlic. Place cooked cauliflower into the bowl and add olives and capers.

To make the dressing, blend olive oil, lemon juice, sugar, mustard, salt, pepper, and garlic. Pour it over the cauliflower and mix well. Serves 4–6.

Minted Salad

1 green bell pepper
1 red bell pepper
4 tomatoes
2 cucumbers
8 radishes
1 small hot pepper (optional)
3 scallions, finely chopped

1 clove garlic, crushed
1 tablespoon fresh parsley, finely chopped
1 bunch stemmed fresh mint, finely chopped
4 tablespoons extra-virgin olive oil
2 tablespoons lemon juice
Salt and pepper to taste

Dice first six ingredients into very small cubes. Add scallions, garlic, parsley, and mint. Toss in salad bowl. Blend olive oil, lemon juice, salt, and pepper; pour over salad. Serves 6.

Avocado, Grapefruit, and Orange Salad

2 avocados
3 oranges, segmented
2 grapefruit, segmented
1 red bell pepper, cut in strips

4 tablespoons extra-virgin olive oil
2 tablespoons lemon juice
Salt and pepper to taste
Paprika to taste

Peel and cut avocados into wedges. Remove membranes from grapefruit and orange segments. Arrange in a circle, alternating colors. Garnish with red pepper. Blend oil, lemon juice, and seasoning. Pour over salad. Serves 4.

Lobo Earns His Santa Suit

Lobo Bielich waited five years for his first return visit to Peru, his South American home, to see his two brothers and their young children. Lobo had worked hard in the New World and had done very well for himself. Now he looked forward to seeing his little nieces and nephews—and he looked forward to a spectacular mission: he was to play Santa Claus on Nochebuena.

His brothers had told him that there was no one they could rely on to play Santa Claus because their kids were too sharp and could easily spot any of their relatives lurking behind the white whiskers. But they had never seen Lobo, the rich uncle who lived in the far-off country of America. Nor were they told he was coming for Nochebuena.

Lobo got himself outfitted with the perfect Santa suit and rehearsed his "Ho, ho, ho!" to perfection. The plan couldn't fail. He would park behind a nearby church and carry his toy-laden bag two blocks to his brothers' homes, which were on the same street. He would enter the first brother's house, cause a big sensation, and leave his toys under the tree. Then, still shouting "Ho, ho, ho!" he would leave the enthralled children and walk across the street to the other brother's house where he would repeat the performance.

It was a cold night and a frost had been forecast when Lobo pulled his rented Fiat into a parking space behind the church. Struggling with his big bag of toys, he hoisted them at last onto his back and began the two-block trudge to his brother's house, hurrying a little so as to arrive on time.

But at the front of the church, he was stopped short by an all-too-familiar scene. Huddled around a fire on the church steps were two small Indian children and their gaunt mother, a threadbare blanket around their shoulders. They looked cold, miserable, and sad.

When they saw Lobo coming from behind the church, the children's eyes lit up.

"Santa! Santa! Santa Claus!" they squealed in excitement. The mother, wise in the ways of the street, shushed the children. She knew Santa's toys were not for her kids, but she hoped Santa could spare some change.

Trapped in his Santa Claus outfit, Lobo had neither his billfold nor any change, and he certainly couldn't give away the gifts meant for his nieces and nephews. With a breaking heart, Santa put his head down and marched resolutely toward the first brother's house.

But now his heart was not in it. His thoughts kept going back to the expectant looks on the faces of the Indian children. As he practiced his "Ho, ho, ho!" it lacked conviction. He felt empty and drained of Christmas spirit.

He stopped at a red light, waiting to cross the street. There was not a car in sight. It had grown late. Lobo felt the chill of the Nochebuena frost, and he shuddered, stamping his feet to keep them from freezing. It was taking a long time for the light to change, and he had just about made up his mind to cross anyway, when a dilapidated old Volkswagen drove up, stopping right in front of him.

The car was covered with dust. Lashed down with rope, two pieces of cheap luggage and a cage holding two chickens teeter-tottered on the roof of the car. A cloud of white exhaust rose from the battered old exhaust pipe.

Santa's Dilemma.

pacheco
97

Suddenly, on the passenger side of the car, the face of a five-year-old boy popped up. His eyes grew wide as he beheld Santa Claus. He yelled to his little brother, "Anselmo! Wake up! It's Santa Claus!"

A second little boy appeared, rubbing the sleep from his eyes, which soon turned to huge black saucers. "Sí, sí. Es Santa Claus!" The little boy danced up and down in the back seat. The older boy pressed his nose and fat cheeks against the pane of the front window.

The light went to yellow—in thirty seconds it would be green and they would be gone. Santa Claus could continue on his way, deliver the toys to his nieces and nephews, and be done.

"I told you Santa Claus would come," the older boy said to his little brother.

"He didn't forget us," said little Anselmo, also pressing his nose flat against the window.

With that, Lobo had had enough. He reached into his bag, grabbed the biggest toys he could find, and, hoping that he had chosen toys for boys, opened the door of the Volkswagen and handed the toys to the children.

This time, Lobo's "Ho, ho, ho!" had the hearty ring of truth to it. At the wheel, stunned speechless, the father could only wave his gratitude as he inched the old Volkswagen forward.

Lobo stood on the corner for a few minutes, feeling pretty good about the whole Santa Claus business. He hefted his bag, two presents lighter, onto his back and started off.

At his brothers' houses, Santa Claus was a huge hit. He played his role to the hilt. The kids were amazed and never guessed that Santa was in reality their rich Uncle Lobo from America, and they never noticed that two of the presents remained in his big bag.

After the merrymaking, Lobo could not wait to get back to the front of the church. He almost ran all the way for fear that the mother and two children would be gone. But he was in luck.

The two children were asleep, covered with the one ragged blanket. The fire sputtered fitfully for lack of wood. The woman looked up at Santa Claus but said nothing.

Quietly, Lobo put a gaily wrapped gift in the arms of both Indian girls. The next day they would know that there actually *was* a Santa Claus.

Lobo had borrowed a few bills from his brother and had taken a plate from the overflowing Nochebuena table. These he handed to the Indian mother without a word. She accepted it without ever changing expression.

"Gracias. Que Dios te bendiga," she said. ("Thanks. May God bless you.")

"He already has," said Santa Claus, feeling like he had done a good night's work. It was the best Nochebuena that Lobo had ever had.

Bicicleta the Scrooge

Bicicleta was a gaunt man who lived by pushing his tired, rickety bicycle through the alleys of Ybor City (hence the nickname "Bicicleta"). He picked clean the garbage cans of Ybor City, taking a bit of thread here, a refundable bottle there, discarded appliances, scraps of metal, cloth, and buttons, and in this way he made his living, such as it was.

I came to know Bicicleta as a customer at my father's pharmacy, La Economica Drug Store, where he was extended privileges commensurate with his rank of Miser Extraordinaire. The Miser never bought anything for which he had no immediate need, and he never spent more than fifteen cents. For example, he only bought one aspirin at a time. Bicicleta's thinking was that if he bought aspirin like everyone else, in quantities of twelve, and then died the next day, he would have left behind eleven unused aspirins—an intolerable waste. Plus there was the penny profit to be considered. My father would sell Bicicleta one aspirin for two pennies. A box of twelve Bayer's aspirins cost twenty-five cents. Hence, buying them at two pennies each ultimately saved him a penny. Of such savings are fortunes accumulated!

The facts are nebulous, but somewhere in Ybor City, Bicicleta had a wife. I never met her, nor met anyone who ever had, but the fact remains that Bicicleta and his wife produced a son. It was this son who demanded that Bicicleta buy him a new Ford convertible when he graduated from high school. One day when the old miser was in to buy his five cents' worth of boric acid powder, I asked him why he permitted his son to waste his hard-earned money.

With his answer, the disheveled, threadbare old man expanded my definition of the word *miser*. He smiled his gap-toothed smile and said, "He'll never have as much fun spending my money as I had saving it."

When I began to collect Nochebuena stories, I didn't think of Bicicleta, who had long since died. I thought I had heard the last of Bicicleta the Miser. But when it comes to the stories of Ybor City, there are always more. While shooting the breeze at the Tropicana Coffee Shop, I heard a new one about the Miser.

It was almost Christmastime, but Bicicleta was surely not going to give his one-year-old son a Christmas toy. The infant didn't even know it was Christmas and would not appreciate the gift. The second year was touch and go, but finally Bicicleta gave in to his miserly instinct and did not give his son a gift that Christmas either.

By the third Christmas, however, Bicicleta recognized his obligation and began early his diligent search through the garbage cans of Ybor City. Months before Christmas he came across a toy horse with a broken wheel. It was frayed and cuffed and the paint was chipped and dull. Gleefully Bicicleta seized it, strapped it to his bicycle, and took it home to repair and restore it.

The horse was basically a broomstick, on one end of which was a carved piece of wood resembling a horse's head. On the other end was a wheel that allowed the horse to roll on the sidewalk. The reins were a simple piece of white rope.

Bicicleta was crafty and good with his hands, so the horse, once finished, was wonderful—no doubt better than it had been new. The boy was ecstatic with his toy and for an entire year was seen every day around his block, riding his horse. It was conceded that Bicicleta had done right by his son.

The fourth Christmas presented a problem for Bicicleta. Try as he might, he was not able to find a gift in the garbage cans of Ybor that could match the horse. The boy even slept with it. Christmas was fast approaching and Bicicleta had no idea what he would do for a gift. Desperation seized him.

Then one evening, as the winter sun was setting and he trudged home through the penumbral gloom of the alley, Bicicleta seized on a solution.

Four days before Christmas, the beloved horse disappeared. The boy cried and cried, and everyone made a big show of finding it, but, no, it was gone. The boy was shattered. Bicicleta tried to comfort his son, assuring him that he had a straight line to Santa Claus, and that he was positive Santa would bring the boy a new and better horse.

Of course Bicicleta outdid himself in refurbishing the old horse, which he had stolen and hidden from the boy. He repainted the head and found two huge blue buttons from off a lady's overcoat to use for the eyes. A clean, white, unused mop, discarded because its handle had broken, provided him with the horse's new mane and tail. He found a bigger wheel for the back, and, by sheer luck, came across a leather strap from a woman's shoulder bag to use for the reins.

The four-year-old boy was beside himself with joy. Bicicleta told him that this new horse was named Trigger, and that made him even happier.

From here on I leave it to the powers of Ybor City storytelling to determine the story's end. The old man who told it to me went on to say that Bicicleta pulled off the same stolen-horse gag for three more Christmases. Some others sitting around our table said no, it was four—and they had never even heard of Bicicleta until that morning!

However it ended, the story provided closure for me. I'd always wondered why Bicicleta's son had insisted that his father buy him a new Ford convertible. Now I saw the full circle of logic. That boy understood that his father had bamboozled him out of at least four Christmas gifts, and it was payoff time.

Meats

Rib Roast

1 7–9 lb. rib roast
½ tablespoon salt
1 tablespoon chopped garlic
1 tablespoon fresh rosemary

1 tablespoon fresh thyme
1 tablespoon fresh marjoram
1 tablespoon pepper

Preheat oven to 375 degrees. Trim fat from rib. Mix seasonings and rub all over meat. Place in roasting pan, insert a meat thermometer, and roast at 350 degrees for 2½–3½ hours. An internal temperature of 110 degrees will produce a rare roast; 120 degrees, medium-rare; and an additional 10 degrees for each increasing level of doneness desired. In all cases, remove roast from oven and let stand ½ hour before carving. Serve with horseradish sauce. Serves 15.

Glazed Baked Ham

1 15–18 lb. ham, uncooked
1 cup brown sugar, packed
2 teaspoons dry mustard
3 tablespoons apple cider vinegar

1 teaspoon whole cloves
Orange or pineapple slices, for garnish
1 24-oz. jar spiced red apples, for garnish
1 bunch parsley, for garnish

Preheat oven to 325 degrees. Unwrap ham and run cold water over it. Dry with a cloth and place in a roasting pan. Insert meat thermometer on fat side, into thickest part of ham. Bake uncovered, allowing 20 minutes per pound, until thermometer registers 160 degrees.

Remove pan from oven. Cut rind off ham and score fat diagonally, in diamond shapes. In a bowl, combine brown sugar, mustard, and vinegar; spread over top of ham. Insert cloves at points where diamond lines intersect.

Return ham to oven and increase heat to 425 degrees. Bake 15 minutes, or until sugar forms a glaze. Remove from oven and place on a large platter. Garnish with fruit slices and parsley. Serve with raisin sauce (see p. 88). Serves 20–25.

Sicilian Sausage

Sausage casing
7 lbs. boneless pork butt or shoulder, trimmed of fat and ground to medium thickness
7 teaspoons Italian parsley, chopped
7 teaspoons fresh oregano
2 cloves garlic, crushed

3 teaspoons anise seed, crushed
7 teaspoons fennel
½ cup Romano cheese, grated
3 teaspoons salt
3 teaspoons pepper

Mix ground pork with parsley, fennel, oregano, garlic, anise seed, Romano cheese, salt, and pepper. To stuff casing, use a long funnel with a nozzle about 1 inch in diameter. Tie a secure knot in one end of the casing, fit the open end over the funnel's nozzle, and pull the casing until the nozzle reaches the knotted end.

With a clean needle, poke a hole in the knotted end to allow air to escape as you stuff meat into the casing. Push meat into casing with your hands until it has all been used. Tie a knot in open end. Refrigerate for 1 hour.

Place sausage in a roasting pan in preheated oven at 375 degrees. Cook 15–20 minutes, until golden brown. Serves 8–10.

Sausage with Peppers and Potatoes

4 large potatoes, unpeeled, medium-diced
3 green bell peppers, thinly sliced
3 large onions, peeled, thinly sliced
5 lbs. Italian sausage, sliced
   1–2 inches thick

½ cup dry white wine
2 tablespoons extra-virgin
   olive oil

Boil potatoes in water 10 minutes. Set aside. In a large skillet, sauté peppers and onions in oil until tender. Add potatoes and sausage; cook until sausage is brown. Add wine. Simmer until wine evaporates. Serves 8–10.

Meatballs

1 lb. ground beef
2 eggs
½ cup Italian seasoned bread
3 tablespoons fresh parsley, chopped

2 tablespoons fresh oregano,
   chopped, or 1 teaspoon dry
   oregano crumbs
1 tablespoon garlic powder
4 ozs. water (optional)

In a large bowl, mix beef with eggs and bread crumbs. Add herbs and mix. If too dry, add water. Using an ice-cream scoop, make round balls about 1½ inches in diameter. Place in a roasting pan and bake at 375 degrees until well done. Serves 6.

Leg of Veal

1 6-lb. veal roast
¼ cup extra-virgin olive oil
1 large onion, chopped
1 bay leaf
½ teaspoon cumin

1 tablespoon salt
1 teaspoon white pepper
½ cup burgundy
2 tablespoons lemon juice
1 sprig parsley

Preheat oven to 350 degrees. While oven is heating, heat oil in a roasting pan. Over high heat, sear roast thoroughly on all sides, about 10 minutes. Lower heat to medium. Add onion, bay leaf, and cumin, sautéing with roast until onion becomes limp. Add salt, pepper, wine, lemon juice, and parsley.

Insert a meat thermometer in center of roast, taking care not to touch the bone. Cover and place in oven. Roast 2¼ hours at 350 degrees. The meat should cook until the thermometer reaches a temperature of 175 degrees. Uncover and raise oven temperature to 400 degrees to brown, about 15 minutes. Let stand 15 to 20 minutes. Spoon juice from roast over the meat. Serves 6.

Leg of Pork

1 teaspoon oregano
5 cloves garlic, chopped
1 tablespoon salt
½ teaspoon pepper
4 tablespoons extra-virgin olive oil
1 5-lb. leg of pork
8 pimiento-stuffed olives, halved

2 teaspoons capers, drained
1 onion, chopped
1 green bell pepper, chopped
½ cup dry white wine
Juice from 6 sour oranges (or 3 oranges and 3 lemons)

PREPARING THE ROAST AND MARINADE

In a small bowl, mash oregano and garlic together. Add salt, pepper, and olive oil. Mix well and set aside.

With a sharp knife, make several slits on surface of pork. Move knife from side to side to enlarge pockets. Rub herb mixture into each pocket and all over the roast. Place in a roasting pan.

In a bowl, mix together olives, capers, onion, and green pepper; sprinkle over roast. Combine wine and sour orange juice; pour over roast. Cover and refrigerate 2–3 days. Turn 3 or 4 times a day.

Preheat oven to 325 degrees. Remove roast from pan and pour marinade into a bowl. Return roast to pan and insert a meat thermometer into pork, taking care not to touch the bone. Cover. Roast 45 minutes, without basting. Then uncover and continue roasting, basting with marinade every 15–20 minutes, until marinade is used up. The roast should cook until meat thermometer registers 175 degrees, 40–45 minutes to the pound. Remove from oven. Let stand 15–20 minutes before carving, until meat reaches a temperature of 155 degrees. Serves 6.

GRAVY

While roast is standing, strain juices from the roasting pan into a saucepan. Cook over low heat until juices are reduced by ⅓, or to the consistency of your taste. When meat is done, slice and spoon hot gravy over it. Serve remainder in a gravy boat.

Lechón Asado Vasco
(Basque Roast Suckling Pig)

1 8-lb. suckling pig
1 tablespoon salt; 1 teaspoon salt
2 cups fresh white bread crumbs
2 tablespoons milk
4 medium onions, chopped
½ lb. ground pork
½ lb. ground veal
1 liver of suckling pig, chopped
2 tablespoons parsley, chopped
1 teaspoon dried thyme
1 teaspoon dried rosemary

½ cup dry sherry
¼ cup brandy
2 eggs, beaten; 6 eggs, hard-boiled and sliced
½ teaspoon pepper, freshly ground
1 small potato, for garnish
2 cherries, for garnish
1 small red apple, for garnish
Red bell peppers, for garnish
Green bell peppers, for garnish
Dark-green watercress, for garnish

Wash pig under cold running water; dry inside and out. Rub with 1 tablespoon salt. To prepare stuffing, put the bread crumbs in a large bowl and moisten with milk. Add onions, ground pork, veal, and liver. Add herbs, sherry, brandy, and beaten eggs. Season with salt and pepper and mix thoroughly.

Preheat oven to 400 degrees. Line inside of pig with hard-boiled egg slices. Fill with stuffing. Run a skewer through both sides of the opening, lacing with string to close. Put raw potato in pig's mouth and place aluminum foil over its ears and mouth, to prevent blackening. Roast for 2¾–3 hours at 400 degrees. Baste with pan juices and additional olive oil, if needed.

When the pig is done, transfer it to a platter. Remove skewers, lacing, and foil. Replace potato with apple. Place cherries in the eyes. Serve with thin gravy made from skimmed pan juices. Whole roasted red and green peppers and dark-green watercress are often used as garnish. Serves 8–10.

Roast Lamb, Castilian Style

3–4 lb. leg of lamb, or 3–4 lbs.
   leg pieces, preferably shank portion
2 tablespoons lard
Salt and pepper to taste
¼ teaspoon paprika
1 clove garlic, crushed
2 cups water
2 cloves garlic, peeled
3 slices onion

1 bay leaf
2 sprigs parsley
2 tablespoons vinegar
¼ teaspoon rosemary
¼ teaspoon oregano
¼ teaspoon ground cumin
Juice of 1 lemon
¼ teaspoon salt

Preheat oven to 450 degrees. Place lamb in a roasting pan and rub with lard. Sprinkle with salt, pepper, and paprika. Rub in garlic. Roast 15 minutes.

After 15 minutes, bring remaining ingredients to a boil in a saucepan.

Lower oven temperature to 350 degrees. Pour ½ cup of saucepan mixture over meat and continue roasting, 12–20 minutes to the pound, depending on desired doneness. Baste every 10 minutes, replenishing liquid in saucepan with more water, if necessary; keep simmering while lamb is roasting.

Slice lamb and serve with remaining liquid. Serves 3–4.

Lechón Asado Estilo Cubano (Cuban Roast Suckling Pig)

1 whole suckling pig, about 60 lbs.
4 tablespoons salt
20 garlic cloves, crushed, plus
   extra for rubbing pig

Juice of 15 sour oranges or 20 lemons
4 tablespoons oregano
2 tablespoons pepper

Preheat oven to 375 degrees. Clean the pig by washing it under cold running water and drying inside and out. Rub salt and crushed garlic on all sides; pierce the skin all over and insert 5 cloves of garlic into the holes (a little in each hole). In a bowl, make marinade by mixing citrus juice, oregano, salt, pepper, and 15 cloves garlic. Transfer pig to a large baking pan. Using a brush, baste with marinade on all sides. Let stand 3 hours.

Place pig in preheated oven and reduce temperature to 350 degrees. (If whole pig does not fit, cut in half; when the pig is cooked and roasted, put back together.) Bake a minimum of 6 hours, turning upside down after 3 hours. Baste occasionally with marinade. When the pig is cooked through, add more marinade. Raise oven temperature to 450 degrees and roast 15 minutes longer to brown. Remove from oven and transfer to a large serving platter or board. Slice meat from the meaty parts, such as the leg and loin, and include crackling skin with each portion. Serves 40.

Monteria para Navidad
(Pork Leftovers for Christmas Day)

2 onions, chopped
2 green bell peppers
1 cup vegetable oil
8 garlic cloves, crushed
1 8-oz. can tomatoes, crushed
1 cup green olives
1 cup raisins

1 cup capers
1 bay leaf
¼ teaspoon pepper
Ribs and pieces of cooked pork
3 cups water
2 teaspoons salt
1 cup dry white wine

In a large pan, sauté onions and peppers in oil until brown. Add garlic, tomatoes, olives, raisins, capers, bay leaf, and pepper. Add pork, salted water, and wine. Cook over medium heat 15 minutes. Serve with roasted potatoes.

Fresh Pork Ham

1 6-lb. fresh pork ham
1 cup sour orange juice (if unavailable, ½ cup lemon juice and ½ cup orange juice)
½ teaspoon salt

8 large cloves garlic, chopped
2 teaspoons oregano
¼ teaspoon pepper

Wash ham and pat dry. With a sharp knife, puncture holes in several places. Place in shallow roasting pan. Pour juice over ham and rub salt on it. In a bowl, mash garlic, oregano, and pepper into a smooth paste. Rub all over pork, making sure that mixture is pushed into holes. Marinate 6–8 hours or overnight. Preheat oven to 350 degrees. Bake ham skin side up for about 3 hours. (For a 6-lb. ham, allow 30 minutes per pound; for hams that weigh 10 or more lbs., allow 20 minutes per pound.) Let ham stand at room temperature for 30 minutes before carving. Serves 8.

Brisket of Beef

3–4 cloves garlic, minced
1 teaspoon salt
1 teaspoon pepper, freshly ground
2 tablespoons vegetable oil

6–7-lb. whole brisket, lean (first cut)
2 onions, chopped
4 carrots, peeled and sliced into coins
1 cup dry red wine, water, or chicken broth (see p. 38)

Begin preparations the day before dinner. Preheat oven to 350 degrees. Make a paste of garlic, salt, and pepper, and rub all over brisket. Heat vegetable oil in roasting pan on top of stove; sear brisket on both sides over medium-high heat, about 15 minutes. Remove brisket to platter.

Scrape bottom of roasting pan to loosen searing juices and particles. Place onions in pan, then brisket on top of onions, carrots on top of brisket. Pour wine, water, or chicken broth into pan. Cover tightly with aluminum foil. Bake for 2–2½ hours, until meat is tender.

Remove meat and carrots from pan and place on a platter. Pour pan liquid and onions into a bowl. Cover platter and bowl with plastic wrap and refrigerate. The next day, remove congealed fat from onions. To make gravy, push the liquid, onions, and carrots through a food mill or sieve.

Cut brisket into slices ⅛–¼ inch thick. Return meat to roasting pan. Spoon gravy over meat, reserving some for gravy boat. Place meat in 350-degree oven 10–15 minutes, until heated through. Excellent with potato latkes (see p. 195). Serves 8–10.

Fruited Pot Roast

4–5 lb. chuck roast
1 24-oz. can whole tomatoes, with liquid
1 16-oz. can pitted apricots, with syrup

2 medium onions, sliced
1 cup mixed dried fruit
    (pitted prunes, raisins,
    apricots, peaches, pears, etc.)

Place meat in a small roasting pan. In a large mixing bowl, combine tomatoes and canned apricots with onions and dried fruit. Pour mixture over meat. Bake, covered, in a 325-degree oven for 4 hours, until roast is fork-tender. Remove pan from oven and let meat cool. Refrigerate.

When the meat-fruit sauce has congealed, skim off all fat. Reheat pot roast and sauce, and serve immediately. (May also prepare weeks ahead and freeze.)

To serve, slice meat and arrange on a platter. Top with onions and fruit from sauce. Pour sauce into a gravy boat. Serves 8–10.

Sauerbraten

MARINADE

2 cups vinegar	1 bay leaf
2 cups water	1 carrot, sliced
1 tablespoon salt	1 onion, sliced
¼ teaspoon pepper	3 stalks celery, shredded
12 peppercorns	2 cloves garlic

In a deep pan, bring vinegar and water to a boil with salt, pepper, peppercorns, bay leaf, carrot, onion, celery, and garlic. Simmer 15 minutes. Let cool.

POT ROAST

1 4-lb. rump or sirloin roast
2 tablespoons vegetable oil
2 medium-sized onions, chopped
2 large tomatoes, peeled and chopped
1 cup beef broth (see below, or use bouillon cube)

1 tablespoon sugar
Juice of 1 lemon
1 cup red wine
¾ cup raisins

Wipe meat with a damp cloth. Put in a casserole dish and pour marinade over meat. Cover with plastic wrap and marinate 4 hours, turning periodically. Drain meat and strain marinade.

Heat oil in a large pot over high heat and brown meat 5 minutes on each side. Add onions, tomatoes, broth, sugar, and lemon juice. Moisten with wine and 1 cup of marinade. Cover with a tight-fitting lid and gently simmer 3 hours, adding more marinade if needed. A half-hour before meat is done, add raisins. Sauerbraten goes well with latkes (see pp. 195–96). Serves 8–10.

BEEF BROTH

1 flank steak (about 1½ lbs.)
2 large onions, quartered
1 green bell pepper, cut in strips
6 garlic cloves, crushed

2 tomatoes, quartered
1 bay leaf
1 carrot
Salt to taste

Cut flank steak into 4 x 4 inch pieces. Place in stockpot, cover with water. Boil; skim foam off surface. Add remaining ingredients, cover, and boil until beef is tender. Strain.

Stuffed Breast of Veal

5 lbs. breast of veal
4 cups water
1 cup dried apricots or
    1½ cups pitted prunes
4 cups soft bread crumbs

¼ cup vegetable oil, plus extra for
    basting
2 tart apples, sliced
½ teaspoon salt

Have butcher bone and cut pocket in veal breast. Soak dried apricots or prunes in hot water for 20 minutes. Drain, saving liquid. Chop soaked fruit. Using a fork and tossing lightly, combine bread crumbs, oil, apples, and salt. (For moister dressing, use a little liquid left over from soaked fruit.) Stuff mixture into veal pocket.

Roast on rack in roasting pan, covered, at 325 degrees, for about 2½ hours, allowing 25–30 minutes per pound. Baste occasionally with a little more vegetable oil. Serves 8–10.

Sweet Potato and Prune Tzimmes

1½ lbs. pitted prunes
2 lbs. brisket of beef
1 teaspoon salt
¼ teaspoon pepper

6 medium sweet potatoes
½ cup sugar
1½ tablespoons lemon juice

Soak prunes several hours or overnight in cold water to cover. Combine prunes, water from soaking, and meat in a heavy pot. Season with salt and pepper. Bring to a boil and simmer over very low heat until meat is almost tender, about 1½ hours. Remove meat and prunes from gravy. Add sweet potatoes (peeled and sliced). Place meat and prunes on top of potatoes and sprinkle with sugar and lemon juice. Cover and bake at 350 degrees for about 40 minutes, until potatoes are tender and meat is browned. Serves 6.

A William Tell Nochebuena

When Roland Manteiga was ten years old, he was taken to spend Nochebuena with the Rodriguez family. In the late 1920s, Roland's father, Don Victoriano Manteiga, was considered one of the most famous men of Ybor City because of his prominence as the editor of *La Gaceta*, the community's trilingual newspaper, and as a *lector* (reader), one of the highly respected men employed by the cigar factories to read to the cigar makers as they labored. While the popular Don Victoriano skipped about the city visiting one Nochebuena table after another, Roland and his mother, Ophelia, were happy to settle in one home and enjoy a quiet and sumptuous repast.

One of the benefits of visiting the Rodriguez home was that Roland got to play with the three children, George, Albert, and Rainier. Albert was ten, Roland's age, and the two had been close playmates since they were very young boys.

It was the Rodriguez family's habit to put all of the children's toys under the tree before Nochebuena, since the three boys knew the truth about Santa Claus, making subterfuge unnecessary. While the women of the family bustled about the kitchen putting the finishing touches on the Nochebuena feast, and the men drank their brandies, smoked their cigars, and talked politics, the kids scouted out the toys under the tree.

One gift that had been too big to wrap properly was easily identified as a bow and arrow set. Too excited about this gift to wait, the boys quietly removed it from under the tree and took it out to the back yard, where they set up the target under the large oak tree. But the target was a floppy piece of work, so someone had to stand next to it and hold it so that it wouldn't fall over. It was decided that Roland should take the first turn as target holder. At the appropriate moment, he would step aside as each of the Rodriguez boys took his turn shooting at the target.

The first shot was given to Roland's pal Albert. Almost immediately it occurred to Roland that this was perhaps not a wise choice. Albert was cross-eyed. Until such time as a cross-eyed friend points a steel-tipped arrow at a target next to which you are standing, it does not occur to you that such an event is fraught with unpleasant possibilities. But what was Roland to do?

He had only just time enough to yell, "Concentrate on the target, Albert! Just remember you are cross-eyed!"

Roland Manteiga as a young cowboy.

But Albert had released his arrow already, and it found its target perfectly. Roland flopped over onto his back, the arrow lodged right between his eyes. The three Rodriguez brothers stood paralyzed, their mouths open, not knowing if Albert had killed their friend or not.

At the sink in the kitchen, Roland's mother had happened to glance out the window just as her son keeled over in the grass. She ran shrieking from the house and, without hesitating, pulled the arrow out of her son's head. Fortunately, it had barely penetrated the skin. Furious, Mr. Rodriguez demanded to know which of his sons had shot the arrow. Like true brothers, all three clammed up, and from where he lay in the grass, Roland weakly protested that his wound had been self-inflicted.

Roland grew up to succeed his father as editor of *La Gaceta,* and he became the driving force in the restoration of Ybor City. On that Nochebuena, he learned two lessons he would never forget: always stand by your buddy, and always stand *behind* a visually impaired person who is shooting at a target.

Manteiga's Bull's-Eye.

Gravies and Sauces

Turkey Giblet Gravy

½ cup all-purpose flour
1½ cups melted turkey drippings
3½ cups turkey or vegetable broth
  (see p. 38)

Turkey giblets, cooked
1½ teaspoons salt
⅛ teaspoon pepper

Pour drippings into saucepan, and blend in flour. Gradually add broth and cook over low heat, stirring constantly, until thickened. Add remaining ingredients and heat to serving temperature, stirring constantly. Makes 4 cups.

Raisin Sauce for Ham

1 cup raisins
¼ cup butter
½ teaspoon lemon juice
1 tablespoon cornstarch

½ cup apple juice
⅛ teaspoon cinnamon
Sugar to taste (about 1 tablespoon)

Mix raisins, butter, and lemon juice in a saucepan and simmer until raisins are tender. Add cornstarch, sugar, cinnamon, and apple juice; continue cooking to desired thickness. Serve over ham slices.

Hollandaise Sauce

¼ cup melted butter
2 tablespoons lemon juice
3 egg yolks, well beaten

⅛ teaspoon salt
½ cup butter
⅛ teaspoon cayenne pepper

Combine ¼ cup melted butter, lemon juice, egg yolks, and salt in top of double boiler. Cook over hot water, beating constantly, until butter melts. Add remaining ½ cup butter and cayenne; cook, stirring constantly, until thickened. Serve immediately, with fish or vegetables. Makes about 1 cup.

Pommarola
(Basic Tomato Sauce)

10 lbs. very ripe fresh tomatoes, or 2 2-lb.
    cans peeled Italian plum tomatoes
2 cloves garlic, finely chopped
2 tablespoons light extra-virgin olive oil

1 teaspoon salt
½ teaspoon black pepper
1 tablespoon minced fresh
    basil, or 2 teaspoons dry basil

Peel fresh tomatoes, remove seeds, and dice. If using canned tomatoes, press through a sieve.

Put garlic in a saucepan with olive oil and simmer over low heat until garlic is light brown. Remove garlic with a slotted spoon and discard. Swiftly pour tomatoes into saucepan. Add salt, pepper, and basil and cook over low heat, stirring frequently with a wooden spoon, until well blended. Continue to cook and stir, uncovered, until most of the water has evaporated and sauce has thickened, about 30–40 minutes. Makes 7–8 cups.

Bolognese Sauce

2 slices bacon, chopped
1 tablespoon unsalted butter
3 tablespoons chopped prosciutto
1 medium onion, chopped
2 carrots, finely chopped
2 stalks celery, chopped
½ lb. lean beef, ground
½ lb. veal, ground
¼ lb. lean pork, ground
1 cup chicken broth, fresh (see p. 38) or canned
1 cup dry white wine
3 ripe tomatoes, peeled and diced, or 2 cups canned Italian plum tomatoes, chopped
1 teaspoon salt
Pepper to taste
1 clove garlic, crushed
¼ teaspoon grated nutmeg
1 cup hot water
½ lb. mushrooms, sliced
½ cup light cream

In a large pot, cook bacon in butter until soft; add prosciutto and simmer 4 minutes. Add onion, carrots, celery and cook until soft, about 10 minutes. Add beef, veal, and pork; stir until red has disappeared and meat is broken up into small pieces. Add broth and wine and cook until sauce thickens, stirring constantly. Add the tomatoes. If canned, press through a sieve. Add salt, pepper, garlic, and nutmeg; stir well. Taste for seasoning. Add hot water, cover pan, and simmer over low heat for 1 hour, stirring frequently. Add mushrooms and cook, uncovered, for 10 minutes. Just before serving sauce add cream. Stir well, bring to boil once and take off heat. Serve over pasta. Makes 5 cups.

Marinara Sauce #1

6 scallions without tops, chopped
6 garlic cloves, chopped
¼ cup extra-virgin olive oil
1 32-oz. can tomatoes, crushed
1 32-oz. can tomato sauce
1 carrot, scraped and coarsely chopped
8 sweet basil leaves, or ½ teaspoon dried basil
Salt and pepper to taste

Sauté scallions and garlic in olive oil until limp; add crushed tomatoes, tomato sauce, carrot, basil, salt, and pepper. Cook, partially covered, for approximately 1 hour. Serve over pasta. Makes about 2 quarts.

Marinara Sauce #2

6 scallions without tops, chopped
1 teaspoon garlic, minced
¼ cup extra-virgin olive oil

3 lbs. plum tomatoes, peeled and
 seeded
8 sweet basil leaves

Sauté scallions and garlic in olive oil until limp. Process tomatoes in food processor until coarsely chopped. Add to scallions and garlic. Add basil and boil gently, partially covered, for 30 minutes. Makes about 4 cups.

Mojo Salsa
(Cuban Garlic Sauce)

8 garlic cloves
1 teaspoon salt
1 medium onion, thinly sliced

½ cup sour orange juice, or ½ cup
 orange juice and ¼ cup lemon juice,
 combined
½ cup extra-virgin olive oil

Crush garlic with salt in a mortar and pestle or in a food processor until it forms a smooth paste. Combine garlic, onion, and juice in a bowl. Heat oil in a skillet, add mixture, and stir for 3 minutes. Serve heated, with meats. Makes 1 cup.

Chimole
(Chili Sauce)

1 tablespoon vegetable oil
1 medium onion, finely chopped
1 clove garlic, peeled and minced
1 teaspoon chili powder

1 large tomato, peeled, seeded, and
   coarsely chopped
1 cup beef or chicken broth (see pp.
   82, 38)
Salt to taste
Black pepper, freshly ground, to taste

Heat oil in a small, heavy-bottomed saucepan and sauté onion and garlic over low heat until golden. Add chili powder and mix well. Add tomato and cook over low heat, stirring from time to time, until the mixture is thick and almost dry. Stir in broth, bring to a boil, reduce heat and cook sauce gently for about 10 minutes. Season to taste with salt and freshly ground pepper. Makes 1 cup.

Applesauce

8 cooking apples
½ cup water
⅛ teaspoon salt
½ cup sugar

Wash, pare, and core apples. Add ½ cup water and ⅛ teaspoon salt. Cook in covered pot until soft. Add ½ cup sugar, simmering just long enough to melt sugar.

Note: Amount of sugar and water varies with sweetness and juiciness of apples. For additional flavoring, add sugar, nutmeg, cinnamon, grated lemon rind or juice, to taste.

Nochebuena and the Fortunes of War

Angel Rieira was a strange little man and a wonderful musician. Unfortunately, he liked good wine a little more than good music, and he had been drinking steadily ever since his years spent as a soldier in the Spanish Civil War.

Angel played in the most famous of all Spanish show orchestras, Los Chavales de España, which was how I met him. I was courting the beautiful Luisita Sevilla, who was the band's featured flamenco dancer. It was December, we were in New York, and Angel was a wonderful storyteller. So one night very near Christmas, in between sets, I got him to tell me the story of a Nochebuena long ago, in 1938, when fate and his music had saved him from death at the hands of Franco's Nationalist Army.

The battle for Teruel was over by early November of 1938. The Loyalist forces had gambled on a big offensive and lost. By November 15, they had fallen back to the Ebro River and suffered heavy casualties crossing it. By December 23, Franco's Nationalist Army was mounting its final offensive in Catalonia, headed for Barcelona and the end of the bitter, bloody war.

Rieira, Jimeno, Martinez, Bona, and a fat drummer, Pablo, were members of a regimental band in Spain's Loyalist Army. Teruel had been a harsh experience, and a cold one—so cold the trumpet player could not even put his lips to the metal of his mouthpiece. The crossing of the Ebro had also been a disaster; there Rieira had lost his precious violin. His last glimpse of it was as it floated down the swift Ebro alongside a dead machine gunner's body.

It was Rieira, the band's leader, who decided that they should desert. All were Catalans, a fierce people who distinguish themselves vehemently from the Spaniards, and so they felt right at home with the peasants of Catalonia, who looked with suspicion on anyone who spoke Castilian Spanish rather than Catalan. With the peasants' help, the small band managed to sneak away from the defeated army and take to the hills using little-known back roads.

It was just a week before Christmas and the cold was intensifying when Angel and his men turned down a dusty side road leading to Barcelona. They were hungry, tired, and freezing.

As they got farther away from the fighting, they felt safer, but fear propelled them constantly forward, toward Barcelona, where Rieira and Pablo, the fat drummer, both lived. If caught at a Loyalist checkpoint, they would all be executed. So on they went.

At last, in the distance, Rieira spotted a farmhouse which looked strangely silent. When the ragged band hit the top of the hill and looked down at the farm below, they understood why. The farmer and his wife lay face down in the field, probably strafed by an Italian Fiat fighter plane while they worked.

They rushed into the house and built a fire. The cupboards were filled with potatoes, onions, eggs, and other goods. Pablo immediately whipped up an omelet of potatoes, onions, peas, and Serrano ham.

With full bellies, the boys sat by the fire warming themselves, and promised each other they would wake the next morning and bury the poor farmer and his wife, who still lay face down in the field. They sang a few old Catalan songs and then went to sleep on the hard floor in front of the fire.

The house was quite adequate for its day, boasting electricity, running water, and a two-holer outhouse right outside the back door. It was hard to leave such comfort, and the boys voted to stay a few days to rest and recover their strength.

In the farmer's bedroom, they discovered a radio. Hardly able to believe their good fortune, they tuned in to hear *both* the Loyalist and the Nationalist news. Neither was particularly reassuring. The Loyalists had fallen back to Barcelona, and the army was quickly becoming a rabble. Angel and his men wanted no part of *that* debacle. Meanwhile, the Nationalists were advancing without much opposition. Germans, Italians, and Moors led the vanguard of the Spanish Foreign Legion. That news froze them in fear. It meant that up the very road that led to their farmhouse, tanks, trucks, cavalry, and infantry would soon come and capture them. They would meet one of two fates: immediate execution or, at a minimum, ten years of hard labor in a POW camp. Neither fate seemed particularly appealing.

It was during the close of the Nationalist Army's broadcast that Angel Rieira had his brainstorm. What if his band of musicians learned the Nationalist government's national anthem? What if they divested themselves of their uniforms, put on the dead peasants' clothing, and went out to meet whatever military force was coming down the road? Could any commander get mad at a bunch of musicians who knew Franco's national anthem?

To put Angel's plan into action, they would have to wait until the next night, when the radio played the anthem again. Then, each of the musicians would have to memorize a bar or two and write it down hurriedly.

Their rehearsals would be haphazard, since not one of them was schooled enough to write out the notes properly—they all played by ear. Rieira was designated as the one who would try to remember the entire piece by ear. Each of the others would listen only to the part played by his own instrument.

It went badly. It was already December 23, almost Nochebuena, and they could not produce a sound that anyone might identify as Franco's anthem. But luck took a tiny turn. As Franco's advance became a tidal wave, the Loyalist radio stations fell along the way, and as soon as they fell, the Nationalist Army, with its dearth of deejays, had nothing to play, so they played recordings of the national anthem over and over again, between recordings of Franco's speeches.

By December 24, the boys could play a decent version of the national anthem, and they looked forward to celebrating Nochebuena as Nationalist soldiers.

At midday, Martinez, who was on sentry duty, came running down the hill, the brightly colored quilt he wore as a cloak flapping in the wind.

"They're coming!" he yelled, "A colonel on a huge white horse!"

"Line up!" roared Rieira, his sax at his lips. "Boys, make this as good as you can, and make it LOUD."

"But we don't know the bridge yet," said Bona, the trumpet man.

"Skip the bridge," Rieira said. "Just play what we know—over and over and over—until they hire us or kill us."

As soon as the fine white head of the Arabian stallion appeared over the rim of the hill, the band struck its first thunderous, if ragged, chord. The horse shied, and the rider, a tall, beautifully uniformed colonel, pulled his mount to rein and rode toward the musicians.

The Moorish soldiers behind the colonel seemed agitated. They pointed to the musicians and pulled out their long, curved knives, indicating with

Bona Hits a High C.

broad strokes what they would like to do to them if permitted by their colonel. The band played harder and louder.

The colonel pulled up in front of the band, laughing. "Ya basa! Paren!" (Enough! Stop!).

Rieira waved the band to a ragged stop.

"What is this?"

"Your regimental band, my Colonel. We are all Catalans, and we want the honor of accompanying your magnificent army into Barcelona."

The colonel laughed again and turned to a major on horseback behind him. The major's scarred face was contorted into a permanent grimace. *He* wasn't laughing.

"These are obviously Loyalist deserters," said the major.

"Sí, per supuesto, but . . ." The colonel hesitated.

"But we have our orders. We shoot any deserters we catch on this road, sir."

"Sí, sí. But we do need a band. After all, who in Franco's army will have music? I will enter on my fine white Arabian stallion, alone in front, followed by you and the other officers, and then—my regimental band! The people will go wild. They've been waiting to see my killer Moors, and now we will herald their victorious entrance with music!" The colonel laughed again, and Rieira thought he had never seen a high-ranking officer laugh so much in his life. He was either crazy, or drunk, or both.

"Thank you, Sire!" Rieira said. "We will rehearse, we will play music as you have never heard! These men of mine may seem a motley bunch to you, but they are all first-rate musicians. Bona! Play a high C."

Bona stepped forward, put his lips to the ice-cold mouthpiece of his trumpet, and hit a C that reverberated in the hills, its echo spooking both the horses and the Moors.

"So it is settled. We camp here and celebrate Nochebuena tonight, and you will play me a *jota,* and an *aragonesa,* and a *sevillana* . . ."

Rieira lifted his glass. "So we entered Barcelona at the head of a column of Moors. My mother saw me, and they say she suffered a minor stroke."

Rieira stood up shakily, for he had been drinking steadily during the telling of his Nochebuena story. Those at the tables closest to us applauded Angel, for they had been listening.

"Well, to work!" he said.

And then he went up onstage, played through "Madrileña" faultlessly, and went on to play Lecuona's "La Comparsa" very well, never missing a note, even when he fell, head first, onto a table of Japanese tourists below.

Saint Anthony and the
Two Miracles of Christmas

That Christmas was a miraculous time has been evident to me ever since I was a child, growing up in the home of my grandfather Gustavo Jimenez, the Spanish consul. How else to explain the huge, elaborately decorated Christmas tree and displays in our living room? How else explain the overwhelming abundance of exotic foods on our Nochebuena table in the middle of a harsh economic depression? Or the stream of friendly, gift-bearing citizens and friends? Or the stacks of toys and new clothes?

Surely Christmas is a time for miracles. You just have to know how to appreciate them. They're not always so easy to spot, you know.

Since my marriage to Luisita and the birth of our daughter, Tina, we have experienced two such miracles. All families have their favorite Christmas stories. Some are sad, some funny, some are moving. This is a pair of related Christmas stories that have greatly affected our daughter Tina's growing awareness of this holy day and its true meaning.

Saint Anthony Lends a Hand

The winter of 1961 was bitter and especially hard for young Karen Louise Maestas, called Luisita. After years of training which culminated in two final years of study in Seville, Spain, she had arrived at her goal: to be considered a great and promising young flamenco dancer. Now it was her desire to seek employment in New York City.

Her mother, Margo, had recently moved to New York to help her other daughter, Kathi, who was divorced and struggling to support herself and her two babies in the big city. So Luisita, Kathi, and Margo were reunited in New York that year in December. Christmastime found this small family crowded into a two-room apartment at the 1–2–3 Hotel on West 46th Street. Margo, a bright and hard-working woman, pounded the pavement daily looking for work, while Luisita made the rounds auditioning for different dance troupes. But day after day, failure and unemployment was their shared fate. The money, so carefully hoarded, was at last running out. Christmas week looked dim.

Then Margo landed a job at Rockefeller Center with Kenny Corporation. On the day of Christmas Eve, she went to her first day of work. Although she didn't even have money for lunch, she didn't feel that she had a right to ask for an advance, even if it was Christmas Eve and her need was desperate. Uppermost in her mind were her two little grandchildren. A very religious woman, Margo trudged through the streets filled with joyous Christmas shoppers to Saint Patrick's Cathedral. She found the statue of Saint Anthony, patron saint of the poor and friend to the needy, and kneeled to pray.

Margo Maestas.

"Please, Saint Anthony, I am not asking for myself. I am asking for my grandbabies. They need milk. I want you to tell me what to do. I did not ask to be put into this position, and all I need is two dollars and twenty cents—two dollars for milk, and two dimes for the fare to get home to them." And then Margo lit a candle and repeated her request three times. She returned to work.

When Margo got off work that evening, the snow was falling fast. She knew it would be very difficult for her to walk the long way home in the swirling snow, and she was mindful that she still did not have the two dollars she needed to buy another day's worth of milk for the babies. A strong feeling compelled her back to Saint Patrick's Cathedral.

Once inside, she stayed a long time, again kneeling before the statue of Saint Anthony. "My babies need milk, and I can't bear to go home without it. Please hear my prayer and answer me." When she looked up, it seemed to Margo that the face of the statue looked different.

It was snowing even harder when Margo left Saint Patrick's, forcing her to go slowly and carefully down the long steps so as to avoid falling. And then, in a golden moment, she saw it in the snow. Right at her feet was a bright green coin purse. She looked both ways to see if there was anyone who might claim it. Trembling, she snapped open the purse and emptied the contents into her palm. Inside were two crisp dollar bills and two shiny dimes.

There have been many wonderful Christmas days in the Maestas family, but none so memorable as the day when Saint Anthony reached out to help them to survive one more day. It was their first miracle of Christmas.

Saint Anthony Speaks Again

After the trial of that difficult Christmas, the luck of the Maestas family changed dramatically for the better. Kathi remarried, and she and her children returned to Denver, as did Margo. Luisita, whose fresh beauty and pure talent could not be long overlooked, at last found work in the world of flamenco, and from that point forward she could be confident that she would never lack for anything, so long as she could dance.

By a wonderful turn of fate, Luisita's troupe traveled to Miami to perform and, in a series of serendipitous encounters, found happiness in an unexpected place—a doctor's office. When we met I was a practicing physician in my early forties, and Luisita Sevilla, the flamenco dancer, was only twenty-eight. We decided very quickly to marry. It proved to be one of the great, lucky decisions of my life.

We settled into a wonderful, warm home and together we had a beautiful little girl who looked very much like her mother—a child who has brought us every great happiness and joy. Little Tina proved to be a perfect child, free even from the usual childhood illnesses. Every stage of her development was likewise, problem-free. She sped through her early years, and her laughter filled our home. Our lives seemed complete. But into every happy home there comes the occasional dark cloud.

It was December. I had launched a new career as a boxing commentator for NBC, and I had to go to New York to cover a fight. Tina was seven—the perfect age for an introduction to the beauty and excitement of New York at Christmastime—so we all went together.

Three years earlier, while doing a *jota* in a performance, Luisita had torn the cartilage in her knee. The doctors had recommended surgery, but it was a risky enough procedure that they couldn't guarantee she would dance again. On the other hand, if she didn't have surgery, she risked doing very real and permanent harm to herself. To Luisita, it seemed an impossible decision. She loved dance almost as much as she loved me and Tina. It was a part of her. How could she willingly submit to a surgery that might put an end to one of her greatest joys in this life? Luisita's decision was complicated by an inner conflict. The time spent recuperating had given her more time to spend with her husband and young daughter. Perhaps giving up dance was what she was supposed to do.

It was a delight to watch Tina eat ice cream at Rumple Meyers, play at F.A.O. Schwarz, and have lunch at the Plaza Hotel (just like her favorite heroine in her favorite book, *Eloise*). But whereas Tina and I were in seventh heaven, the normally ebullient Luisita seemed to be under a dark cloud. Her knee was bothering her again. Should she have the surgery? And if she had it, would she ever dance again?

On the afternoon of Christmas Eve, I left Tina and Luisita to enjoy the afternoon together while I attended meetings. With the story of Saint Anthony's first miracle fresh in her mind, and the worry of her knee heavy on her heart, Luisita decided it was time for a visit to Saint Patrick's Cathedral.

She told Tina that she wanted to see Saint Anthony and thank him. Tina had heard the story of Saint Anthony so many times that her curiosity was aroused. She wanted to see this miracle-working statue. Luisita believed deeply in Saint Anthony, but Tina, even at that young age, was skeptical.

Once at the church, Luisita lit her candles, kneeled before the statue, and prayed. First she thanked Saint Anthony for her mother's first miracle. Then she asked him to help her make a decision. Should she have the surgery? Would she still be able to dance? Or did God mean for her to give up dance forever?

Once again, as on that desperate Christmas Eve so many years ago, it was snowing hard when Luisita and Tina made their way out of the cathedral. The crowds on the sidewalks below them leaned into the strong, driving winds. It was a nasty day, but their hotel was only a few blocks away, so Luisita decided they should walk. Tina's hand clutched tightly in her own, Luisita began her careful descent down the slippery steps. Suddenly, she fell very hard, her knee locking so that she could neither straighten nor bend it. She could not stand. She lay helpless on the cold, wet steps. Tina tried to lift her, to no avail. Passersby hailed a cab and a nearby Santa Claus quit ringing his bell to help her. In the silence of the cab, with only the sound of her mother's pain-wracked sobs, Tina put things into perspective: "Well, Saint Anthony certainly didn't help you, Mom."

But Luisita knew that Saint Anthony had answered her prayer. Now she was forced to make the only decision she could: to have the surgery, no matter what the outcome.

This Nochebuena story has a happy ending, for Luisita's surgery was a great success, and she is still able to dance and teach. It was our second miracle of Christmas.

Fish and Seafood

Flounder with Crabmeat Stuffing

2 tablespoons extra-virgin olive oil
½ cup onions, finely chopped
1 cup mushrooms, thinly sliced
¼ cup celery, finely chopped
½ cup green pepper, finely chopped
3 cloves garlic, chopped
4 fresh basil leaves
⅛ teaspoon Tabasco sauce

1 teaspoon salt
¼ teaspoon pepper
4 flounder fillets
Juice of ½ lemon
½ lb. crabmeat
2 sprigs parsley, finely chopped
¼ cup white wine
¾ cup bread crumbs

To make stuffing, heat oil in a large skillet over high heat and sauté onions, mushrooms, celery, green pepper, and garlic. Add basil, Tabasco sauce, salt, and pepper, and cook 5 minutes more. Add crabmeat, parsley, wine, and bread crumbs; cook an additional 5 minutes. Remove from heat.

To prepare flounder, place 2 fillets in a baking pan. Sprinkle with lemon juice. Spoon stuffing on 2 fillets, and place other 2 fillets on top of stuffing. In a 350-degree oven, bake 25 to 35 minutes, until the bottom layer of fish flakes easily when tested with a fork. Serves 4.

Crab Rolls

CRABMEAT MIXTURE

2 onions, finely chopped
1 green bell pepper, finely chopped
1 8-oz. can tomato sauce
1 clove garlic, finely chopped
1 tablespoon extra-virgin olive oil
1 bay leaf

1 teaspoon salt
1 teaspoon pepper
1 teaspoon Tabasco sauce
½ teaspoon sugar
½ teaspoon nutmeg
1 lb. crabmeat (claw)

In a saucepan, sauté onions and green pepper until transparent. Add remaining ingredients except crabmeat. Mix well. Cover and simmer ½ hour. Add crabmeat and continue cooking 10 minutes. Let cool. Refrigerate for 1 hour.

BREADING

1 cup bread crumbs
2 tablespoons all-purpose flour
½ teaspoon salt
½ teaspoon pepper

Mix ingredients well in a bowl.

MAKING THE CRAB ROLLS

2 eggs, lightly beaten with 2 tablespoons water
Vegetable oil for frying

For each crab roll, shape 1 tablespoon crabmeat mixture into a ball. Roll in breading, then in egg, and again in breading. Refrigerate 2 hours. (*Note:* May be frozen instead of refrigerated, then defrosted and fried.) In a large skillet heat oil about ½ inch deep. Fry crab rolls over medium heat until golden brown. Can be kept warm in 200-degree oven until needed. Serves 4.

Italian Red Snapper

¼ cup extra-virgin olive oil
2 onions, chopped
2 green bell peppers
6 cloves garlic, mashed
1 16-oz. can tomato sauce
1 28-oz. can Italian crushed tomatoes
1 bay leaf
8 leaves fresh basil, chopped,
    or 1 teaspoon dried basil

1 teaspoon oregano
3 tablespoons fresh parsley,
    chopped
1 cup red wine
Pinch of sugar
Salt and pepper to taste
5-lb. red snapper
2 medium Idaho potatoes
Vegetable oil for frying

In a large skillet over high heat, sauté onions and peppers, then garlic, in olive oil for 5 minutes, until onions turn translucent. Lower heat to medium and add tomato sauce, crushed tomatoes, herbs, wine, sugar, salt, and pepper. Cook another 10 minutes. Lower heat and simmer sauce 30 minutes.

While waiting for sauce, scale and gut red snapper. Sprinkle additional salt and pepper in abdomen. Set fish aside.

Peel potatoes and slice into rounds. Fry in vegetable oil until golden brown but not fully cooked through. In a baking pan, arrange potatoes in a layer, pour some of the sauce over them, place snapper on top, and pour rest of sauce over fish. Cover with aluminum foil and bake in preheated oven at 350 degrees for 40 minutes. Remove foil and continue baking 10 minutes, or until fish flakes easily when tested with a fork. Serves 6.

Lobster with Vanilla Mayonnaise

2 lbs. cooked lobster meat, or 4 lobster tails
4 cups cold water
1 teaspoon salt; ½ teaspoon salt

3 large egg yolks
½ vanilla bean, chopped, or 2
    teaspoons vanilla extract
1½ tablespoons fresh lemon
    juice

½ cup olive oil   ⅛ teaspoon white pepper
1 cup canola oil   Watercress sprigs, for garnish

If using lobster meat, skip to third paragraph. If using lobster tails, bring cold water to a boil. Add 1 teaspoon salt. Drop lobster tails in. Cook 5 to 8 minutes, until bright red. Remove, drain, and cool. Remove tail from shell and strip out the vein that runs along the back. Refrigerate 1 hour.

To make vanilla mayonnaise, combine oils and set aside. Put egg yolks into a blender at low speed until well mixed. Keep blender going and add oil mixture a few drops at a time in a slow, steady stream. As emulsion begins to thicken, add oil a few more drops at a time, but be careful not to add too much too soon. When the emulsion is thick, add vanilla. Continue blending. In a small bowl, stir ½ teaspoon salt into lemon juice. Slowly add juice to emulsion. Turn off blender. With a thin plastic or rubber spatula, scrape off any remaining oil and stir gently into the mayonnaise. Add pepper.

Slice lobster tails or meat into ½-inch-thick medallions; if using tails, return to shells. Place on a cool plate with 2 tablespoons mayonnaise beside each lobster portion. Garnish with watercress. Serves 4.

Baked Fish with Lemon and Dill

6 white fish fillets (about 1½ lbs.)   1 clove garlic, minced
½ cup white wine   ¼ teaspoon salt
Juice of 1 lemon   Lemon slices, for garnish
2 tablespoons fresh dill, chopped   Dill sprigs, for garnish

Fold fish fillets into thirds and place in a baking pan. Combine wine, lemon juice, dill, and garlic, and pour over fish. Bake in a 350-degree oven 20 to 25 minutes, or until fish flakes.

Place fillets on a serving platter and sprinkle with salt. Garnish with lemon slices and dill sprigs. Serves 6.

Trout with Mushrooms

6 trout, about 10 ozs. each
1 teaspoon salt
1 teaspoon pepper
½ cup all-purpose flour
1 tablespoon extra-virgin olive oil
2 tablespoons butter

2 tablespoons white wine
2 scallions, finely chopped
3 cups mushrooms, sliced; mushrooms for garnish
Juice of ½ lemon; lemon quarters, for garnish
1 tablespoon fresh parsley; parsley sprigs, for garnish

Wash trout, leaving heads and tails on, and pat dry. Season inside and out with salt and pepper. Coat lightly with flour. Heat oil and butter in a large skillet. Sauté trout 6 to 8 minutes on each side, until lightly browned.

In another skillet, heat wine. Add scallions and mushrooms, and cook over medium heat for 3 to 5 minutes, until mushrooms begin to soften. Add lemon juice and parsley. Toss lightly.

Place trout side by side on a large platter with rows of mushrooms between them. Garnish with lemon and parsley. Serves 6.

Fillet of Sole with Shrimp and Artichokes

3 lbs. sole fillets
24 medium raw shrimp
½ cup lemon juice
½ teaspoon white pepper
1 teaspoon Italian seasoning
4 tablespoons butter
1 large onion, chopped
½ lb. mushrooms, sliced

⅓ cup dry vermouth
16 frozen artichoke hearts, thawed
1 teaspoon salt
½ teaspoon black pepper
1 cup tomato purée
⅓ cup low-fat milk
1 small jar pimientos, chopped
½ cup parsley, chopped

Cut sole fillets into strips, about 1 x 2 inches. Shell and devein the shrimp. In a large bowl, mix lemon juice, salt, white pepper, and Italian seasoning. Add sole and shrimp; marinate 1 hour in refrigerator. Stir occasionally. Drain well.

In a large skillet heat 2 tablespoons of the butter. Add onion, mushrooms, salt, and black pepper. Sauté 5 minutes over medium heat. Add tomato purée, vermouth, sole, and shrimp. Simmer 5 minutes. With a slotted spoon, remove fish onto a heated platter.

Heat remaining butter in a saucepan. Add artichoke hearts. Cook 5 minutes over low heat. Add tomato mixture and bring to a boil. Reduce by about ⅓. Add milk and pimientos to finish sauce. Simmer 2 minutes.

Spoon up shrimp and arrange on top of sole. Cover with sauce. Garnish with chopped parsley. Serves 8.

Mussels in Vermouth

48 mussels
1 cup dry white vermouth
8 shallots or 1 small onion, chopped
1 tablespoon butter
2 teaspoons cornstarch

½ teaspoon salt
¼ teaspoon pepper
½ teaspoon fennel seed
2 tablespoons parsley, chopped

Wash and scrub mussels and place in a skillet. Add vermouth and shallots or onions. Cover and cook over high heat 4 to 6 minutes, or until mussels open. Remove mussels with a slotted spoon and keep warm.

Add butter and cornstarch to vermouth sauce in skillet. Cook over medium heat until sauce thickens slightly. Add salt, pepper, fennel, and parsley. Bring to a boil. Serve mussels with sauce in soup plates. Serves 6.

Spanish Red Snapper

1 5–6-lb. red snapper, filleted and scaled
8 garlic cloves, mashed
3 onions, thinly sliced
1 teaspoon oregano
Juice of 3 lemons
1 teaspoon salt

3 potatoes, peeled
3 tomatoes, sliced
1 cup extra-virgin olive oil
¼ teaspoon pepper
Parsley, for garnish
Salt to taste

Wash snapper inside and out. Pat dry. Make two diagonal slits on each side. Using a mortar and pestle or a food processor set on high, make a paste of garlic, oregano, and pepper.

Place fish in a long, shallow roasting pan. Drench with lemon juice on both sides and inside. Sprinkle salt inside and out. Rub outside of fish with garlic mixture, inserting part of it into slits. Refrigerate 2 hours.

Preheat oven to 350 degrees. Just before baking fish, parboil potatoes (cover with water and boil over medium heat about 8 minutes); cut into ½-inch-thick rounds. Lift fish from pan and set aside. Pour ½ cup olive oil in bottom of pan. Arrange layers of potatoes, onions, and tomatoes, and place snapper on top. Drizzle rest of olive oil on fish. Bake at 350 degrees for 1 hour and 15 minutes. Salt to taste. Decorate with parsley. This recipe works well for any whole whitefish. Serves 6.

Asturian Fish Mélange

1-lb. red snapper fillet
1-lb. flounder fillet
1-lb. halibut fillet or steak
1 lb. medium shrimp, shelled and deveined
16 ozs. raw oysters, shucked (optional)

1 teaspoon bay leaves, crushed
⅛ teaspoon pepper flakes
1½ cups tomato sauce, home-
    made (see p. 89) or canned
1 cup dry sherry
1 cup walnuts, chopped

Juice of 1 lemon
1 large onion, finely chopped
3 cloves garlic, crushed
¼ teaspoon coriander
¼ teaspoon thyme
¼ teaspoon nutmeg

½ cup fresh parsley, finely chopped
1 cup seasoned Italian bread crumbs
1 tablespoon butter
½ cup extra-virgin olive oil
1 5-oz. jar pimientos

Cut fillets into 3 pieces each and place in a large, shallow dish. Add shrimp and oysters. Pour lemon juice over fish and shellfish.

In a bowl combine, onion, garlic, seasonings (coriander, thyme, nutmeg, bay leaves, and pepper flakes), tomato sauce, and sherry. In another bowl mix together walnuts, parsley, and bread crumbs.

Divide seafood mixture into 3 parts. Butter generously a 2½–3-quart ovenproof baking dish. Place a layer of seafood in bottom, pour ⅓ of liquid mixture over seafood, and sprinkle with ⅓ of dry ingredients. Continue layering, finishing with dry ingredients. Pour olive oil over last layer. Slice pimientos and arrange on top. Cover and bake 35 minutes in a 375-degree oven. Uncover and bake 15 minutes longer. Serves 7–8.

Note: You may also add 6–8 ozs. crabmeat, clams, or lobster meat to fish ingredients.

Baked Porgy, Madrid Style

4 ¾-lb. porgies or 1 4-lb. porgy,
  cleaned, heads on
1 lemon, cut in thin wedges
Juice of 1 lemon
½ cup extra-virgin olive oil
3 tablespoons onion, chopped
½ cup tomato sauce, preferably
  homemade (see p. 89)

Salt and freshly ground
  pepper
1 bay leaf
1 cup dry white wine
3 cloves garlic, minced
4 tablespoons parsley, minced
6 tablespoons bread crumbs

Make 4 incisions on each ¾-lb. fish, 2 on each side (about 8 incisions, 4 to a side, if using large porgy). Insert lemon wedges so that only rinds are exposed. Sprinkle fish with lemon juice and let stand 30 minutes.

Meanwhile, heat 2 tablespoons of the oil in a small skillet. Sauté onion until wilted. Add tomato sauce, salt and pepper to taste, and bay leaf. Cover and simmer 15 minutes.

Cover bottom of a roasting pan with 2 more tablespoons of oil. Place porgy in pan, sprinkle with salt and pepper, and brush with remaining oil. Bake at 350 degrees for 5 minutes. Add ½ cup of wine and cook 10 minutes more.

In a small bowl, mix together garlic, parsley, and bread crumbs. Spoon tomato sauce over each fish and sprinkle with the garlic mixture. Pour the remaining ½ cup of wine around the sides of the pan. Bake about 45 minutes longer. Serves 4.

Salt Cod with Parsley and Garlic

1½ lbs. salt cod
⅓ cup extra-virgin olive oil
3 cloves garlic, minced
2 tablespoons parsley, chopped

Soak cod overnight in a pan of cold water, changing water from time to time. Drain, cover with fresh water, and bring to a boil. Drain. Boil again. Drain but reserve the liquid. Remove skin and any bones from cod. Break into small pieces (about 1 inch square) and set aside.

In an earthenware casserole dish, heat oil. Add garlic and cook over medium heat until golden. Add fish and parsley. Cook 5 minutes, stirring gently. Add ½ cup of the reserved liquid. Cover tightly and cook over low heat for 7 minutes, stirring occasionally. Serve in same baking dish. Serves 4–6.

Nochebuena and the Flamenco Blockade

My granddaughter, Alexis, was a precocious child. She delighted me with her fast mind, and I was happy to have her in our home for Christmas, to celebrate with my nine-year-old daughter, Tina. Alexis was four years old, chubby, and very cute. She had never experienced Nochebuena, or Christmas for that matter, because her father was Jewish.

Every Nochebuena we opened our doors to what we called "Orphans of the Storm," a mixed group of entertainers and out-of-towners with nowhere to go to celebrate the holidays.

Alexis wore a pretty red dress, and Tina, five years older, took her by the hand and introduced her to everyone. Alexis was primarily interested in the large Christmas tree. What was under the tree? Who got all the presents? And when would Santa Claus come?

Nochebuena that year was a particularly busy one as extra guests dropped by with friends, and Luisita's well-thought-out seating plans went totally awry. We were almost out of food by eleven o'clock, by which time most of our guests had had the courtesy to leave so that we could begin to clean up the house. Luisita would not go to bed on Nochebuena until the house was spic and span. We put the kids to bed, and with the aid of our maid, Aida, and the bartender, an old Israeli Army colonel named Sherman, we all pitched in. At the bar a few of the harder-drinking guests hung on doggedly.

Luisita had recently befriended a very rich, eccentric, Auntie Mame sort of socialite named Dorita. A Cuban Jew by birth, Dorita was a rapt fan of the flamenco world and was constantly taking starving artists and dancers under her wing, mounting performances, concerts, and so on. Dorita was tall, platinum blonde and beautiful, and always dressed to impress in the most expensive clothing. Wherever Dorita went, she had to be the center of attention. Her usual ploy was to be late for any invitation by at least two hours. Guests invited to Dorita's own house for supper at eight would not be surprised when told by the maid that their hostess had not yet arrived, at nine.

So it was not altogether a surprise, the midnight hour fast approaching, when Dorita appeared at our door, a flamenco troupe, guitarist, *cantor* (singer), and an embarrassed husband in tow. Because our house was carpeted, Dorita had brought two large plywood planks. Pushing the furniture back against the walls, she put the boards in place, ordered food and drink for the troupe, and began a flamenco *huerga* (jam session).

My wife has few weaknesses, but flamenco is one she cannot resist. Luisita was one of the best flamenco dancers in the world, and a gypsy's heart burns strong within her. She joined right in. The maid, also a flamenco fan, gladly fixed plates of food, and Colonel Sherman put out fresh wine bottles.

The few guests who had stayed whooped with glee and settled down on the floor to watch the flamencos enjoy a gypsy Nochebuena. Great was the din that they produced.

Tina and Alexis on Christmas Day after the flamenco blockade.

But I was not amused. We live in a quiet neighborhood, and I knew that once the flamencos started, they would not stop until dawn. What was more, there were two children to consider, nestled warm in their beds, and they would want to get up early the next day. Christmas day was a higher priority than a flamenco *huerga,* by far.

At one o'clock, the *huerga* at full tilt, I went to check on the kids. Alexis was sobbing inconsolably. Tina, with all of her persuasive charms, had not been able to quiet her. I sat Alexis on my knee and patted her gently on the back until her sobs settled into sighs.

"Now, what's the matter?" I said.

"If those people keep yelling like that all night, Santa Claus is going to get scared and not come in," Alexis whispered. Tina, who already knew the truth about Santa Claus, had wisely held her tongue.

In that brief moment I saw red. "Flamencos be damned!" I shouted, and I stormed into the main room. Taking hold of one of the plywood boards, I dragged it out of the house and hurled it out onto the front lawn, toppling flamencos in my wake.

"There are children here waiting for Santa Claus!" I yelled at the astonished Dorita. Luisita stood in open-mouthed amazement, having no idea of the traumas being suffered by little Alexis.

Accustomed to being abruptly evicted, the gypsy troupe picked up their instruments, the remaining plywood board, and every half-full wine bottle they could find. They sailed out the door, the guitarist and *cantor* not missing a beat, Dorita reveling in yet another *escándalo* she had precipitated.

The next morning Alexis woke to find herself surrounded by toys. And, aside from a deeply imbedded fear of flamenco-dancing gypsies, she was able to return unscathed to her quiet home up north, where thankfully, nobody celebrated Nochebuena!

Tina's Nochebuena Defeat
of Muhammad Ali

One Nochebuena in the late seventies, when our daughter, Tina, was four years old and sophisticated in the way that only children often are, we welcomed an unusually large number of people to dinner.

To Tina, Nochebuena was a necessary evil, to be endured until she might reap the benefits of Christmas Day, when she would have her parents all to herself and open the many presents brought by Santa Claus.

This Nochebuena was unusually glamorous in that there was a movie crew in town, so our gathering included Ernie Borgnine and his wife, Tova; Joanne Dru, a movie queen of the fifties; and the Italian producer Salvatore Alabiso, his wife, and their assorted children.

But the jewel in the crown was the presence of Muhammad Ali, heavyweight champion of the world. He came accompanied by his gorgeous wife, Veronica, and that boxing commentator of electric-mane fame, Don King. Our guests were elated and excited, and Ali was his usual gracious self, performing on cue, astounding and amazing the guests with his magic tricks and poetry readings. In another corner, the bombastic Don King was

Tina Beats the Champ.

holding court, making people laugh, and promoting his upcoming fights.

Every room was filled with tables for our guests, and it was just about time to serve Luisita's famous roast pig, and turkey with all the trimmings.

Suddenly everyone became aware that Ali was missing. I figured he was probably taking a walk around the neighborhood. But time flew by, and still no Ali. Concerned, his wife and I hopped into my 1947 Cadillac convertible and took a drive around the subdivision. The search proved fruitless—Ali was definitely missing.

My wife was worried lest Ali miss the meal she had worked so hard to prepare. Ali might be Champion of the Ring, but Luisita was the Champion of the Kitchen, and professional courtesy has to be observed.

We looked everywhere. Passing by Tina's playroom, I heard the familiar tinkling bells of her Pachinco game. I peeked in the room and beheld a sight I never expect to see again, even if I live to be one hundred.

There was Ali, his handsome face a mask of concentration, twirling and twisting the knobs, his huge body hunched over, moving with the same fluid motion he showed in the boxing ring. Time after time, however, he'd finish a game with a disappointing score, and little Tina would push him aside so that she could show him how the game was played. Each time she won, she would clap her hands in gleeful victory, and then it was Ali's turn to receive more humiliation at the hands of a four-year-old.

At six foot four, Ali is a man of gigantic proportions. To see this huge man, seated on one of Tina's little chairs, knees up to his chin, and taking up most of what space there was in the playroom, was heartwarming. He was so absorbed in trying to beat our four-year-old Pachinco hustler, that he was willing to miss Nochebuena supper.

With the realization that he would never beat Tina, Ali finally responded to our frantic supplications, stood, and admitted defeat. The antlike Tina had beaten the elephant, Ali. He picked her up and held her high.

"You the Champ!" he yelled. "You beat the Champion of the Whole Wide World!" He made his champion face. "So now YOU the Champ of the Whole Wide World!"

Tina took it in stride—after all, she had beaten some mighty big people—though none (she admitted later in life) as big as the gentle giant Muhammad Ali.

Pasta and Dumplings

Pasta Fresca (Fresh Pasta)

4 cups all-purpose unbleached flour or, if available, semolina flour
2 tablespoons light olive oil
1 teaspoon salt
1–2 tablespoons warm water
4 eggs, lightly beaten

TO MAKE DOUGH BY HAND

Place flour and salt into a large bowl. Make a well in the center. Break eggs into well. Add oil. Knead lightly 2 minutes in bowl, adding water as needed to make a soft dough. Turn out onto a lightly floured board and knead an additional 5 to 6 minutes, until dough is very smooth. Shape into a ball, cover with an inverted bowl, and let stand 30 minutes.

TO MAKE DOUGH IN FOOD PROCESSOR

Insert steel blade into processor. Blend all ingredients except water in fast, short bursts, until dough begins sticking together. Add warm water by teaspoonfuls, just enough to form a ball of soft dough. Turn out onto a floured board and knead by hand for 2 or 3 minutes, until very smooth. Shape into a ball, cover with an inverted bowl, and let stand 30 minutes.

TO MAKE DOUGH IN PASTA MACHINE

It's certainly easier and great fun to make pasta this way. Roll out dough to a ½-inch thickness. Put through a lasagna, cannelloni, fettuccine, or linguine roller. Follow the directions that come with the machine.

TO ROLL OUT AND CUT THE DOUGH

Divide the ball of dough into 3 parts. On a lightly floured board, roll out each as thin as possible, using a straight rolling pin 2 inches in diameter. Dust rolled-out dough lightly with flour, brushing with a wide pastry brush to distribute evenly. Roll up dough into a loose roll, 2½ to 3 inches in diameter.

For tagliatelle, cut dough into long strips ¾ inch wide; for cannelloni, 4 x 4 inch square strips; for lasagna, 3 x 6 inch strips, ½ inch thick; for linguine, long strips ⅛ to ¼ inch wide, ¼-inch thick. Serves 8–10.

Linguine with White Clam Sauce

¼ cup extra-virgin olive oil
4 heaping tablespoons chopped garlic
1 teaspoon dried oregano
1 teaspoon dried basil
¼ teaspoon salt; salt to taste
½ teaspoon black pepper

32 littleneck clams
1 cup clam juice
1 cup water
1 cup clear chicken broth
  (see p. 38)
4 tablespoons sweet butter
Parsley, chopped, for garnish

Place oil, garlic, oregano, basil, ¼ teaspoon salt, and pepper in a saucepan, over high heat. Add clams. Allow garlic to start turning golden brown, but be careful not to burn it. Add clam juice, water, and chicken broth. Cover and steam over low heat. As soon as clams open, add butter and salt to taste. Spoon over linguine, cooked al dente. Garnish with parsley. Serves 4.

Linguine with Red Clam Sauce

1 14½-oz. can Italian plum tomatoes
¼ cup extra-virgin olive oil
4 heaping tablespoons chopped garlic
1 teaspoon dried oregano
1 teaspoon dried basil
¼ teaspoon salt; salt to taste
½ teaspoon black pepper

32 littleneck clams
1 cup clam juice
1 cup water
4 tablespoons sweet butter
1 cup clear chicken broth
  (see p. 38)
Parsley, chopped, for garnish

Chop plum tomatoes into 1-inch pieces. Place oil, garlic, oregano, basil, salt, and pepper in a saucepan over high heat. Add clams. Allow garlic to start turning golden brown, but be careful it doesn't burn. Add clam juice, chicken broth, and water. Cover and steam over low heat. As soon as clams open, stir in tomatoes, then butter. Cook over low heat 5 minutes, stirring often. Add salt to taste. Serve over cooked linguine. Garnish with parsley. Serves 4.

Rigatoni with Vodka

1 large onion, minced
3 tablespoons extra-virgin olive oil
2 15-oz. cans whole Italian tomatoes, drained and chopped
4 ozs. pancetta (unsmoked bacon), minced
¼ teaspoon salt
⅛ teaspoon pepper
1 bay leaf

½ teaspoon thyme
1 teaspoon pink peppercorns
1 cup heavy whipping cream
½ cup vodka
1½ lbs. rigatoni, cooked and kept warm
Fresh basil leaves, for garnish

In a large skillet, sauté onion in oil until translucent. Add tomatoes, pancetta, salt, pepper, bay leaf, and thyme. Cook 5 to 6 minutes over medium heat, until thickened. Add peppercorns and cream. Bring to a boil, reduce heat to low, and simmer 2 to 3 minutes. Add vodka and rigatoni. Toss well. Garnish with basil. Serves 6.

Fettuccine Florentine

1 1-lb. package green fettuccine noodles
1 tablespoon butter
2 cups low-fat ricotta cheese
2 10-oz. packages chopped frozen spinach, defrosted
1½ cups béchamel sauce (see p. 134)

½ cup grated Parmesan cheese
½ teaspoon salt
¼ teaspoon white pepper
½ teaspoon Italian seasoning

Cook fettuccine as directed on package. Drain well and toss with butter. Preheat oven to 350 degrees. Grease a rectangular 8 x 16 inch baking dish. Spread half the noodles in bottom of dish; cover evenly with all the ricotta.

Squeezing out as much water as possible first, spread spinach over pasta-ricotta layer. Pour half the béchamel sauce over spinach. Sprinkle with Parmesan cheese, salt, pepper, and Italian seasoning. Top with layer of remaining noodles, then remaining béchamel sauce. Bake for 25 to 30 minutes, until slightly browned on top. Serves 8.

Pasta Shells, Neapolitan Style

1 to 2 lbs. large raw shrimp (about 16)
8 cups water
½ tablespoon salt
1 16-oz. box (#22) pasta shells
2 tablespoons extra-virgin olive oil

4 tablespoons butter
1 cup grated provolone cheese
1 cup grated Romano or Parmesan cheese
Additional grated Romano cheese, for topping

Wash shrimp thoroughly. In a large pot, bring water to a boil and add salt. Drop in shrimp. Reduce heat and boil shrimp 6 to 10 minutes, until they turn bright pink. Remove shrimp with a slotted spoon, reserving water. Shell and devein shrimp. Set aside.

Cook pasta as directed on package, using water in which shrimp were cooked, adding oil and more water if necessary. Drain, return to pot, and toss with butter and cheeses. While shells are cooking, prepare following sauce (or make in advance).

SAUCE

14 cooked shrimp
Meat from 2 Florida lobsters or 1 medium
Maine lobster (2 lbs.), cooked
1 6-oz. package crabmeat
1 cup extra-virgin olive oil
4 cloves garlic, halved
¼ teaspoon black pepper

½ teaspoon oregano
½ teaspoon basil
½ teaspoon thyme
⅔ cup minced parsley
2 8-oz. cans tomato sauce
Romano cheese, grated, to
taste

Mince shrimp, lobster meat, and crabmeat. In a saucepan, simmer oil and garlic until brown. Remove garlic with slotted spoon and discard. Add minced seafood, pepper, oregano, basil, and thyme, and simmer 2 to 3 minutes. Add parsley and tomato sauce, and simmer 5 to 7 minutes. Taste and add salt, if necessary.

Add whole cooked shrimp (set aside earlier) to sauce and heat through, 1 to 2 minutes. Remove shrimp from sauce and keep warm. Pour sauce over shells and toss lightly. Arrange whole shrimp on top. Serve with additional Romano cheese at the table. Serves 6–8.

Shrimp Pasta

1 mild onion, minced
2 tablespoons extra-virgin olive oil;
 3 tablespoons olive oil
2 cloves garlic, crushed
4 tablespoons Italian brandy or cognac
⅔ cup heavy cream
½ teaspoon oregano
1 lb. linguine, cooked al dente
½ teaspoon salt

1 cup dry white wine
1 lb. large shrimp, shelled,
 deveined, and butterflied
1 14-oz. can tomatoes, drained
 and chopped
½ teaspoon white pepper
1½ lbs. bay scallops, mussels, or
 small clams

Sauté onion over medium heat in 2 tablespoons oil, until translucent. Set aside. Heat 3 tablespoons oil in a different sauté pan over medium heat. Add garlic and cook 2 minutes, stirring occasionally. Add brandy or cognac and flame (strike a match to the liqueur). Cook garlic-brandy mixture for 1 minute over low heat. Add cream, pepper, salt, and oregano. Cook until sauce is reduced by half. Add sautéed onion, wine, shrimp, and tomatoes. Cook 5 minutes. Add bay scallops, mussels, or clams and cook until they are done (mussels or clams should be opened). For each serving, place a portion of linguine and sauce on a plate, and toss gently, arranging several shrimp and bay scallops, clams, or mussels on top. Serves 4–6.

Pumpkin Tortellini

1 small pumpkin
1¾ cups freshly grated Parmesan cheese
10 amaretto biscotti, finely crumbled
1 tablespoon salt
1 teaspoon pepper, freshly ground

1¾ cups all-purpose unbleached flour
2 eggs
3 ozs. butter
¼ cup sage

Using a sharp knife, cut pumpkin into large pieces. Remove seeds. Place pieces on a foil-lined baking sheet and bake in a preheated 350-degree oven for 30 minutes. Let cool. Remove shell and purée 13 ounces of the flesh in a food processor. Mix purée with biscotti and half the Parmesan. Season with salt and pepper.

Heap flour on a board and make a well in the center. Break eggs into the well, working into flour to form a dough. Knead until smooth and elastic. Roll dough out into 2 sheets of equal size. Place teaspoon-size mounds of pumpkin mixture on first sheet, about 2 inches apart. Top with second sheet, pressing lightly around each mound of filling. Using a 2-inch round cookie cutter with fluted edges, cut out tortellini.

Bring a large saucepan of salted water to a boil. Drop in tortellini. Cook al dente, about 2 to 3 minutes.

Melt butter in a small saucepan. Add sage. Drain tortellini and sprinkle with remaining Parmesan. Drizzle with butter and sage. Serves 6.

Puttanesca (Spaghetti with Anchovies and Olives)

40 calamata olives
¼ cup extra-virgin olive oil
4 heaping tablespoons chopped garlic
6 tablespoons capers

6 anchovy fillets
8 cups coarsely chopped Italian plum tomatoes with basil
4 tablespoons butter
Spaghetti, cooked al dente

Pit and coarsely chop the olives. Heat oil in an 8-inch saucepan. Add garlic, olives, capers, and 3 anchovies (chopped). Sauté until garlic starts turning golden. Add tomatoes and cook over low heat ½ hour. Stir frequently. Add butter, allow to melt, and stir in. Serve over spaghetti al dente. Place 3 anchovy fillets on top (optional). Serves 4.

Note: Do *not* add salt.

Baked Fettuccine

½ lb. ground beef
4 garlic cloves, chopped
4 tablespoons fresh Italian parsley, minced
4 tablespoons chopped fresh oregano
4 tablespoons chopped fresh basil
2 28-oz. cans plum tomatoes
2 8-oz. cans tomato paste
¼ cup red wine
¼ cup extra-virgin olive oil
1½ cups Italian bread crumbs
1½ lbs. fettuccine
6 hard-boiled eggs, sliced
½ cup grated Romano cheese
Pinch of sugar
Salt and pepper to taste
Additional grated Romano cheese, for topping

Brown ground beef and drain off fat. Set aside. For the sauce, sauté garlic, parsley, oregano, and basil in olive oil 5 minutes. Add tomatoes, tomato paste, sugar, wine, salt, and pepper, and cook for 30 minutes, or until a nice sauce consistency. Cook fettuccine al dente, draining with cold water. In another frying pan, heat oil, mix in bread crumbs, and stir until toasted.

In a 10 x 12 inch baking pan, spread half of pasta full length. Cover with egg, ground beef, ½ cup Romano cheese, and half the sauce. Layer remaining pasta (full length) and sauce. Cover with toasted bread crumbs, and sprinkle a generous amount of Romano cheese on top. Place in a preheated oven at 375 degrees for 15 minutes. Serves 6.

White Lasagna

BÉCHAMEL SAUCE

8 tablespoons butter
8 tablespoons all-purpose flour
4 cups milk or light cream

1 teaspoon salt
½ teaspoon pepper

Melt butter in saucepan over low heat. Blend in flour. Add milk or cream, salt, and pepper. Stir over medium-low heat until sauce comes to a boil. It should have the consistency of heavy cream. Cover and place saucepan in hot water to prevent film from forming on top. Makes 4 cups.

NOODLES

4 qts. water
25 lasagna noodles
⅓ cup salt
3 tablespoons butter
1 lb. ricotta cheese

4 cups béchamel sauce
8 tablespoons grated Parmesan cheese
2 cups grated mozzarella cheese (half skim, half whole milk), plus ½ cup for topping
Salt and pepper to taste
Parsley, for garnish

Bring water to a boil in a pot large enough for lasagna noodles to lay flat. Add ⅓ cup salt. Place lasagna noodles in water in batches, crossing them two by two. Stir until noodles begin to soften, about 2 minutes (more than that and the noodles begin to stick together). The noodles must be stirred very gently and almost constantly. Drain each batch in a colander, rinse with cold water, and drain separately on dry towel. It takes 10 to 15 minutes to boil all the noodles.

Cover the bottom of a 9 x 13 inch baking pan with 3 tablespoons butter. Place first layer of noodles around the edge of the pan, half in the pan, half over the edge. Next, place 3 or 4 noodles to cover bottom. Spread half the ricotta over them, then ¾ cup béchamel sauce. Sprinkle with half the Parmesan, half the mozzarella, and salt and pepper to taste. Add a layer of noodles, and repeat the ricotta, béchamel sauce, Parmesan, and mozzarella layers. Place remaining noodles on top, and fold draped-over noodles toward the center. Top with ¾ cup béchamel sauce and ½ cup mozzarella.

Bake at 350 degrees, until cheeses melt and top begins to brown. Let cool 10 minutes. Garnish with parsley. Serve remaining béchamel sauce over individual portions at the table. Serves 8.

Lasagna with Meat Sauce

SAUCE

3 28-oz. cans whole plum tomatoes	10 cloves garlic, chopped
3 6-oz. cans tomato paste	1 tablespoon oregano
4 cups water	3 tablespoons unsalted butter
½ cup extra-virgin olive oil	1½ tablespoons dried basil, or 6
2 tablespoons chopped fresh parsley	leaves fresh basil, chopped

In a bowl, crush tomatoes with your hands. Heat oil in a large skillet and add all ingredients except ground beef. Cook over medium-low heat 1½ to 2 hours.

MEAT

1½ lbs. ground beef	1½ tablespoons extra-virgin olive oil
1½ tablespoons chopped garlic	1½ tablespoons oregano
1½ tablespoons chopped parsley	Salt and pepper to taste

In a bowl, mix all ingredients. Pan-fry until beef is light brown. Remove from heat, drain off excess liquid, and set aside. When cooled, add 1 cup of sauce (above).

RICOTTA FILLING

2 lbs. ricotta cheese
1½ tablespoons chopped parsley, fresh
  or dry
1 tablespoon oregano
2 eggs

1 cup grated Romano or
  Parmesan cheese
Salt and pepper to taste
1 tablespoon basil (optional)

In a medium bowl, combine all filling ingredients and set aside.

MAKING THE LASAGNA

1½ lbs. lasagna, cooked al dente
  with 2 teaspoons salt
½ cup grated Romano or Parmesan cheese

6 hard-boiled eggs, chopped
2½ cups shredded mozzarella
  or provolone cheese

Boil noodles. Preheat oven to 375 degrees. In a baking pan (2 inches high, 9 to 10 inches wide, and 14 to 18 inches long), spread thick layer of sauce evenly, then one layer of noodles. Spread all the meat on top. Sprinkle ½ cup of the shredded mozzarella or provolone evenly over meat. Spoon on thin layer of sauce, spreading evenly. Add another layer of noodles, the chopped eggs, and another thin layer of sauce.

Add another layer of noodles and spread ricotta filling evenly over it. Sprinkle ½ cup mozzarella or provolone over ricotta. Add last layer of noodles, a thick layer of sauce, and ½ cup of Romano or Parmesan.

Bake for 45 minutes. Remove. Sprinkle 1½ cups mozzarella or provolone on top. Place back in oven until cheese is melted, about 20 minutes. Serves 15.

Note: The sauce, meat, and filling can be prepared a day ahead and refrigerated.

Polenta and Sausages

6 cups water
½ teaspoon salt
2⅔ cups cornmeal
1½ lbs. Italian sausages
3 tablespoons butter
1 tablespoon red wine vinegar

Bring water and salt to a boil in a large saucepan. Lower the heat to a simmer and sprinkle in cornmeal, stirring constantly with a wooden spoon. Simmer for 40 minutes, stirring frequently.

Prick sausages with a fork. Melt butter in a skillet. Add sausages and fry slowly for 10 minutes over medium heat, turning from time to time. When they are cooked, drizzle vinegar over them and let it evaporate.

Spoon polenta onto a serving plate. Top with sausages and spoon melted sausage fat over it. Serve at once. Serves 4.

Note: Polenta is the basis of many dishes and can be served with any compatible sauce or sprinkled with cheese. It can also be cooled in a pan and cut in squares or wedges, which may be toasted or sautéed.

Potato Dumplings (Gnocchi)

¾ lb. potatoes
1 cup all-purpose flour
1 egg
1 teaspoon salt
2–3 tablespoons grated onion
2–3 tablespoons grated bread crumbs

Peel potatoes. Grate over a bowl of cold water so that they fall straight into water, to prevent discoloration. Drain well and dry on a cloth. Mix potatoes with flour and rest of ingredients. Using a teaspoon, drop potatoes one at a time into a pan of boiling water. Poach 18–20 minutes, until dumplings float to surface. Drain. Serve with marinara sauce (see pp. 90, 91). Serves 4.

Kugel (Noodle Pudding)

1 8-oz. package egg noodles
5 eggs
½ cup butter
½ lb. cream cottage cheese
½ lb. cream cheese, softened

1 cup sour cream
½ teaspoon vanilla
½ cup sugar
Crumbled graham crackers for
  topping

Cook noodles according to directions on package. Drain. In a large bowl, mix well with rest of ingredients except graham crackers. Put in a 9 x 13 inch casserole dish. Sprinkle graham crackers on top. Bake uncovered for 1 hour at 350 degrees. Serves 8.

Fruit Kugel

1 1-lb. package broad egg noodles,
  cooked, drained, and still hot
¼ cup butter, melted
4 eggs, beaten
½ cup raisins

1 12-oz. jar applesauce
1 14-oz. can crushed pineapple,
  drained
1 10-oz. jar apricot preserves

Preheat oven to 350 degrees. In a large bowl, toss hot, drained noodles thoroughly with butter. Combine eggs, raisins, applesauce, and pineapple, beating until well mixed. Add to noodles and toss gently. Spoon mixture evenly into a greased casserole dish. Spread preserves over top. Bake 45 minutes. Serves 8.

A Playboy Nochebuena

My friend Bob reached the end of the 1950s with a feeling of acute disappointment. His professional life was humming along. His work as a photographer was admired from New York to Los Angeles, and he lived in a nice suburban house in Miami with his wife and child. To all appearances, his life was a happy and successful one. He had done all that was expected of him—but still, it wasn't enough. Something was missing.

It wasn't until a photo shoot on the Bahamian island of Eleuthera that he found the thing that would change his life. In his hotel room he found a copy of a new glossy magazine called *Playboy*. Admiring the photographs, Bob was also struck by the work of the publication's owner and philosopher, a thin, earnest man with a pipe who looked like an Ivy League professor: Hugh Hefner, one of America's first and most prominent advocates of the "me-first" philosophy.

But Bob's epiphany came on the balcony of his hotel room at sunset, when he unfolded the center spread of the magnificent Janet Pilgrim. It was then that Bob saw his future with clarity. He became a glamour photographer.

From that day forward, Bob set about divesting himself of every accoutrement of respectability. First, he divorced his wife, gave her the tract house and custody of their child, and moved into his studio. Then he purchased a lifetime subscription to *Playboy* and placed an order for every back issue of the Hefner canon.

Bob's next step was to buy a jaunty Jungle Jim jacket featuring large patch pockets, a safari-style belt, and assorted hooks and pouches, perfect for carrying his film. Then he traded in his three-button suits and cordovan wingtips for a 120-watt hair dryer and the best styling spray money could buy, as recommended in one of Hefner's lesser-known treatises, "The Epistemology of Hair."

Bob rose to the top of his profession in the 1960s and '70s. His mastery of photography was evident, but his sense of artistry and ability to capture the moment were absolutely unique. His prices rose so precipitously that he could soon afford a condo overlooking the Atlantic Ocean and a Mercedes 450 SL with which to impress his young models.

Bob was blessed with great genes. Perennially young, he was considered the Dorian Gray of the glamour photographers. Sporting an even tan and even white teeth, Bob was trim and fit throughout his thirties and forties. His romantic life consisted of a series of trysts with eighteen-year-old models, each of whom lasted about six months before he moved them on and out with a smile and a gentle shove. Greatly envied by his peers, Bob was also a terrifically likable guy. He lived an exemplary dissolute life and never lorded it over anyone.

In the mid-1990s, however, a traumatic event occurred that again would change Bob's life completely. He turned sixty.

Sadly, Bob began to realize that conversation with eighteen-year-old girls had certain limitations. Even his Jungle Jim jacket had begun to lose its luster. His full, wonderful head of hair was now flecked with gray. His once-smooth, handsome face was now attractively wrinkled. And he found he'd rather take a nap at midday than entertain young ladies.

A few days before Nochebuena, Bob appeared at my house. We were going to lunch. Over our meal, Bob seemed unusually solemn and subdued. Sheepishly, he confessed his dissatisfaction with his theretofore shallow existence. He wanted to find a way to make up for two decades of meaningless self-involvement, and he meant to get started with the Christmas celebrations.

I had practiced medicine in Miami's Overtown ghetto, known as the Swamp, and it was there that Bob declared he would start his new life. His intention was to go down the day before Christmas and distribute cash gifts. I suggested, only half-joking, that he go accompanied by armed guards, but he was determined.

So, on Nochebuena, Bob went to the bank and withdrew three hundred dollars, all in tens, which he stuffed into the big patch pockets of his Jungle Jim jacket. And then he got into his Mercedes 450 SL and drove to Second Avenue and Tenth Street. It was a clear, sunny, chilly Miami morning.

At noon, the street was quiet. Ever since the McDuffie riots, the street had tended to resemble Saigon's main thoroughfare just after the Tet offensive. A few men stood loitering in front of the Longshoreman Pool Hall. A few others stood warming their hands around a fifty-gallon fire drum. They viewed the 450 SL and its slick-looking driver with amusement and mild curiosity.

Bob stopped the car in front of the pool hall and called out to the men standing there. He announced that he intended to give out ten-dollar bills to needy families.

The poolroom emptied out, and Bob's car was mobbed. He felt many hands in his pockets, which were quickly emptied. From the glove compartment, his stock of film and leather-bound address book soon followed, as did the cigarette lighter from the dash, and the Rolex from his wrist. It was when someone produced a screwdriver and stuck it into the corner of the radio that Bob said, "Wait!"

His charitable impulses thwarted, his address book lost forever, and his Jungle Jim jacket ripped to shreds, Bob returned to the safety of his condo to rethink his program for self-redemption. It was shortly thereafter that he married a wonderful woman about his own age. They moved into a modest house in Miami's suburbs, and Bob traded in his 450 SL for a Yugo, giving up his work as a glamour photographer to embark on a new career, photographing sunsets in the Everglades.

Giuseppe's Nochebuena Ark

A few years after the turn of the century, Ybor City received an unexpected influx of new immigrants. These were Sicilians who were fleeing a wave of vigilante terrorism in New Orleans, where a chief of police had been killed, and the Sicilian Black Hand society had been blamed. Eleven Sicilians had been strung up and hanged. The rest fled, scattering throughout the South.

The Sicilians had heard that Ybor City, an immigrant community near Tampa, was flourishing. So they headed to Florida, hoping they would be welcomed there with open arms. Alas, such was not the case.

The Spaniards and Cubans did not want more competition for the jobs in the cigar factories and shipyards. So the Sicilians were relegated to the farmlands and empty countryside beyond 22nd Street, Ybor City's outer limit.

Fortunately, most Sicilian immigrants were of peasant stock and familiar with the ways of farming. The land was cheap, some of it outright free. So the Sicilians farmed, became fishermen, opened dairies, and eventually grew wealthy putting the food on Ybor City tables. In time, they also became powerful financiers, bankers, and active participants in local politics and government, but that is a story for the history books. This story is one that was told all over Ybor.

Giuseppe was one of the first Sicilians to arrive in Ybor City following the New Orleans massacre of eleven of his countrymen. Before coming to the New World, his family had lived for generations in Messina, a seafaring town, and were well known as boat builders. Giuseppe hoped to find plentiful work in Tampa, which was full of shipyards that should easily provide employment for a man of his talents.

But once Giuseppe made it to Tampa, he soon realized he would never be given work as a boat builder. The prejudice of Ybor's first-come immigrants was too great. And so he was relegated to the empty lots behind 22nd Street and told to try to earn his living as best he could from the land.

At first Giuseppe was indignant, and then resigned, and finally he realized that he had no choice in the matter. If he was to bring his wife and small children to America, he had to find a way to succeed.

It took several hard years to establish his small farm. Soon he had bought a few milk cows, a goat herd, and additional acres of rich farmland. When he felt financially secure enough, he built a solid, functional house, with enough bedrooms to accommodate the large family he intended to have. Then he sent for his wife, Josefina, and his two boys, who were now big enough to be of great help.

The family grew to seven children, Giuseppe's farm expanded, his handful of cows multiplied into a thriving dairy business, his goats produced cheese, and his vineyard produced grapes sweet enough to produce a good table wine.

World War I came and went without affecting Giuseppe, and so did the great flu epidemic of 1918. The 1920s started off well enough, with all of Giuseppe's business ventures showing a profit and every one of his family members in good health.

But things began to change when the United States government decided to enact a law prohibiting the manufacture and use of alcoholic beverages. Federal agents appeared at Giuseppe's farm, confiscated all of his wine-making apparatus, and warned him of the danger of making—*or drinking*—red wine.

"Well," said Giuseppe, working himself up into a full Sicilian lather, "How is a man to eat his pasta without Chianti? How is a man to digest his food?"

The G-men shrugged and suggested he switch to Coca-Cola, which made Giuseppe even madder. But the law was the law.

At midyear, Giuseppe began taking the wagon into town and buying lumber. Patiently, he cleared out a nice tract of land half a mile from the house. Neighbors, friends, and even his family assumed he was going to build a bigger family house, or perhaps a new barn for the milk cows. Giuseppe didn't say.

After a few months, Giuseppe announced that he had enough lumber to begin his project. The boys were now young men, and each was assigned a job on the farm so that Giuseppe could dedicate himself to his task. He still had not told his family what that task was, and they knew better than to ask.

One day, Giuseppe rose before dawn and, armed with a tape measure and an armful of drawings, he measured and calculated and figured until he was happy with his decisions. Then he carefully marked out a line in the earth, filling it with white chalk. The lumber lay ready and waiting in carefully marked stacks.

That evening, Giuseppe's wife sent the boys to fetch their father for supper. He had skipped lunch, which was unusual enough, but for him to miss supper too was unheard of, and Josefina was very distressed. In all the years of their married life together, he had never missed a meal.

The boys ran out to their father, but soon stopped short in amazement at the strange pile of wood. What was it? A statue of some kind? Long, curved beams of wood stretched the entire length of the field. The entire apparatus was, moreover, held upright by tilted supports. The boys looked at their father as if he had just lost his head.

"A bin for hay?" asked Aldo, the oldest.

"A new way to tie up cows for milking?" suggested the second.

"A tank for water?" Baby Giovanni asked.

Their father laughed. "No, boys, it is none of these things you have guessed."

"What then?" said the middle son, Berito.

"Ah, patience, patience! You shall see soon enough." And Giuseppe laughed as he herded his puzzled sons in to the supper table.

That night, when the full moon illuminated their bedroom and the silver crucifix gleamed on the wall opposite their bed, Josefina snuggled up to her husband as she had when they were young, and she asked him, "Giuseppe, *ma che cosa*?" (But, what is it?)

And Giuseppe laughed. "Quit tempting me, *caro*, you're getting too close to my price. Patience. Soon you will see."

In two weeks, even from the distance of the 22nd Street trolley, it was clear that Giuseppe was building a ship. Not a small ship for fishing in the bay, but a big ship—the kind the Greeks at Tarpon Springs built to go into the deep waters of the Gulf of Mexico for sponges.

Fellow Sicilian farmers traveled for miles on a weekend to see how crazy Giuseppe was getting along with his great colossus of a ship. While they all went away laughing and shaking their heads, they nevertheless admitted grudgingly that it was, indeed, a beautiful ship.

When the sides of the ship got very tall, Giuseppe built a ladder. Not a scaffold, but a ladder.

The Nochebuena Ark.

And then, every morning, Giuseppe would climb the ladder, pull it up behind him, and lower it into the boat's interior. Thereafter, no one saw him again until nightfall. The sounds of his industrious labors were heard, smoke was seen, and everyone concluded that Giuseppe, master boat builder from Messina, was caulking and tarring the inside of his boat so that it wouldn't leak.

Day after day, for more than a year, Giuseppe worked in seclusion deep inside his boat. Not even his wife or boys were allowed to peek inside. No masts had been put in, no engine had been seen. What was crazy old Giuseppe doing?

And still the family flourished. Giuseppe bought more cows, more goats, built a big new barn, and quietly acquired all the land around their farm. Truly, fortune seemed to shine on Giuseppe and his family.

Then one day, almost two years after Giuseppe had first disappeared into the bowels of his boat, Franco the Snitch, an unsavory Sicilian police informer, made up his mind to find out just what Giuseppe was doing in that boat, which by that time had acquired the name of "Giuseppe's Ark" and was the subject of many rumors and much hilarious speculation.

One night, when Giuseppe was sleeping soundly alongside his beloved Josefina, Franco the Snitch brought over his own ladder and climbed into the Ark.

Inside, Franco found a wine press, an elaborately crafted distillery, and case upon case of Chianti and moonshine. So that was it! He had heard rumors that the Ark was a speak-easy, but he hadn't believed it was possible. For all these months, Giuseppe had been supplying the Sicilians with Chianti for their tables, and the Americans with booze.

It was mid-December in the early 1920s. Guessing correctly that Giuseppe would be at his busiest come Christmastime, Franco the Snitch decided to keep quiet awhile and wait until the moment of peak activity to bring in the Tampa police, thereby insuring that his reward would be a substantial one.

So Franco watched Giuseppe's Ark closely, until it began to remind him of an anthill. In the dark of night, people came and went. It seemed like everyone for miles around was coming to buy Giuseppe's Chianti and moonshine liquor.

Finally, just a few days before Christmas, Franco the Snitch decided to make his move. Once informed, the police were overjoyed. Long the subject of the *Tampa Tribune*'s criticism and jibes, they had finally stumbled onto a bust that would make the front page and be remembered for years afterward. It was decided that the chief of police himself would lead the raid.

And on what better night than Nochebuena? With a little luck they might nab a few politicians and a few of the bolita boys, maybe even a Mafia big shot, God forbid.

Carrying tall ladders, the Tampa police advanced stealthily on Giuseppe's Ark. Through the piney woods and palmetto scrub, they tiptoed. At the signal from the chief, they would all scramble up the ladders, blowing whistles and shouting "You're all under arrest!" at the top of their lungs. The barking of the huge police dogs would add to the drama. It would be a glorious bust.

Once his men were assembled, the portly police chief put his whistle to his mouth and blew a mighty blast. The blue-coated cops ran with their ladders, laying them up against the side of Giuseppe's Ark, and scrambled up like medieval knights assaulting a fortress.

The din was incredible. The cops blew on their whistles and shouted, the police dogs yowled, and from the nearby barn, the donkeys brayed nervously while the goats butted their pens, bleating loudly.

The first man to reach the top was an Irish sergeant who had fought with Teddy Roosevelt's Rough Riders and had missed getting to the top of San Juan Hill. He wasn't about to miss *this* charge—he would be the first man to see into the Ark and loudly pronounce its inhabitants under arrest if it killed him.

"You are all . . ." The sergeant started off well enough, but then stopped abruptly and said nothing more. There was a flood of cops behind him, as eager to get to the top as he had been, and they soon toppled him into the Ark. One cop after another, they all stopped short and stared.

Inside, the Ark was a sight to see. Christmas lights hung flickering from the railings, and a small mast had been raised, making the lights look as if they draped a Christmas tree. The cops looked around them. The Ark was full—not with Chianti and moonshine—but with people. A hundred Sicilian peasants sat smiling, grouped around tables, as if waiting for their Nochebuena dinner to be served. At the captain's table sat Don Giuseppe, master shipbuilder, with his proud wife and children.

Giuseppe stood and raised his glass high in a toast. "To America, where even the police snitch on each other!" Amidst great laughter, everyone raised their glasses to toast.

"And to Nochebuena, the eve of the birthday of our savior, Jesus Christ, and a thanks for blessing He brings to this wonderful country of America! Buon Natale!"

To which everyone replied, "Amen!" lifting their glasses high again.

"And lastly, to Coca-Cola, which in the absence of our beloved Chianti, will have to do." And at this, the peasants laughed heartily again and went among the cops passing out wine glasses filled with Coca-Cola.

And so that was the story of the Nochebuena Ark as my Uncle Paul told it each year. The Ark never sailed, but every year during Prohibition, the Italians of Ybor City were assured of having Chianti with which to top off their Nochebuena feast, and without which no Sicilian Nochebuena is ever complete.

Rice and Beans

Spanish Yellow Rice

½ cup extra-virgin olive oil
1 large Spanish onion, chopped
½ teaspoon saffron, or yellow
  vegetable food coloring
4 garlic cloves, minced
4 cups chicken broth (see page 38)
2 bay leaves
2 tomatoes, peeled, seeded, and chopped

2 cups long-grain rice,
  uncooked
2 teaspoons salt
1 medium green bell pepper,
  cut in strips
Green peas, pimiento strips,
  and parsley, for garnish

Heat oil in a casserole dish on a stovetop burner. Sauté onion, green pepper, garlic, bay leaves, and tomatoes over medium heat. Add rice, saffron or food coloring, salt, and broth. Bring to a boil. Lower heat, cover, and cook for 18 minutes, either on top of the stove (low heat) or in the oven (400 degrees). Garnish with peas, pimiento, and parsley. Serves 4–6.

Rice with Raisins and Pine Nuts, Catalan Style

2 cloves garlic, mashed
2 tablespoons peanut oil
2 cups white rice
4 cups water
1 teaspoon lemon juice

½ cup raisins, soaked and drained
1 tablespoon toasted pine nuts or slivered
  almonds
1 teaspoon salt
½ teaspoon ground cumin

In a shallow saucepan, brown garlic in hot peanut oil; do not burn. Discard garlic but not oil. Pour in rice, stir, and add water, mixing thoroughly. Bring to a boil, then reduce heat to low. Add lemon juice, cumin, and salt. Cover and steam 15 minutes. Fluff rice with a fork. Mix in raisins and pine nuts. Serves 4.

Cuban White Rice

2 garlic cloves, mashed
2 tablespoons peanut oil
2 cups long-grain white rice

4 cups water
2 teaspoons salt
1 teaspoon lemon juice

In a shallow saucepan, brown garlic in hot oil until golden; do not burn. Discard garlic but save oil. Add rice and coat thoroughly with oil. Add water, salt, and lemon juice. Bring to a boil, then reduce heat to low. Cover and steam for 18 minutes. Fluff rice with a fork. Serves 4–6.

Black Beans

1 lb. black beans
2 quarts water
2 medium-sized onions, finely chopped;
  plus 1 onion, chopped, for garnish
2 green bell peppers, cut in strips
2 tablespoons extra-virgin olive oil

1 teaspoon oregano, crushed
1 bay leaf
¼ teaspoon ground cumin
4 cloves garlic, minced
1 tablespoon salt
½ teaspoon black pepper

Spread beans on flat surface and discard foreign particles. Wash beans well and soak overnight in 2 quarts water.

Next day, pour beans and soaking water into a 4-quart soup kettle. Bring to a boil. Cover and lower to medium heat. In a skillet, sauté onions and green peppers in oil until light golden color. Blend in crushed oregano, bay leaf, cumin, and garlic. Add to beans in kettle, mixing well. Season with salt and pepper. Continue cooking slowly over medium heat, until beans are tender, about 1½ hours (or about 20 minutes in a pressure cooker). Serve over white rice (see above). Top with chopped onions. Serves 4.

Pinto Beans

2 cups pinto beans, dried
2 ham hocks
1 large onion

2 quarts water
½ teaspoon salt

In a stockpot, cover beans, ham hocks, and onion in water, and bring to a boil. Lower heat and simmer for 4 hours, until beans are tender and liquid is thick. During last hour, season with salt. When done, remove ham hocks and onion. Serves 8–10.

Rice, Mexican Style

2 cups rice
6 slices bacon
½ medium onion
2 green bell peppers
2 cloves garlic
2 sprigs parsley; 2 tablespoons
  chopped parsley, for garnish

3 tomatoes, peeled, seeded, and chopped
1 cup fresh green peas
4 cups chicken broth (see p. 38)
½ teaspoon salt
1 jalapeño pepper

Rinse rice, drain, and spread over a flat surface to dry. Fry bacon in a frying pan and lightly sauté onion, chilies, and garlic in the bacon grease. Add rice and cook until it turns light brown. Add parsley sprigs and tomatoes, stirring constantly. Add peas, chicken broth, jalapeño, and salt. Cover. Let simmer over low heat for 40 minutes. Remove onion, peppers, garlic, and parsley. Garnish with chopped parsley. Serves 4–6.

Rice and Lentils

3 large onions, finely chopped
3 tablespoons extra-virgin olive oil
3 tablespoons pine nuts
1 cup whole brown lentils

4 cups chicken broth (see p. 38)
1 cup long-grain rice
½ teaspoon salt
⅛ teaspoon pepper

In a skillet, fry sliced onions in oil until golden and crisp. Add pine nuts and fry until just golden. Set aside for garnish.

Put lentils in same oil, cover with 2 cups broth, and simmer for about 1½ hours, until lentils are almost soft. Add rice, rest of broth, salt, and pepper. Bring to a boil, reduce heat, and simmer over low heat 15 minutes more, or until moisture is absorbed. Top with fried onions and pine nuts. Serves 6.

Tuto's Last Christmas Fish

Agliano's Fish Market in Ybor City was incredibly busy on Nochebuena day. Since before dawn, the trucks had been delivering the catch of the day. The fish of choice for the Sicilian-Italian community's celebration of Nochebuena (in Italian, La Vigilia di Natale) was red snapper, which was plentiful in Gulf of Mexico waters.

One of the first people in line at Agliano's was a well-known and beloved *bolitero* (a big shot in the numbers racket), whom we shall call Tuto for reasons of self-preservation. The times were hard and getting harder as the Great Depression of the early 1930s ground on—nor was there much reason to hope that it would end anytime soon.

At the rear entrance to Agliano's Fish Market, a second line had formed, and its members stood quietly all through the cold night waiting for Agliano's to open. These were the poorest victims of the depression, waiting to receive fish leftovers and scraps. All were women in threadbare black coats, their faces pinched and gray. At the very back of the line was a thin woman with two small children. Having no one to leave her little ones with, she had brought them along, and they stood obediently, pushing their sleepy faces against their mother's skirts to keep warm.

Whether they got fish heads or tails, these women gratefully accepted Sebastiano Agliano's charity—they thanked him, kissed his hand, and then returned to their homes to make fish soup for their family's Nochebuena dinner. A big, burly man given to loud laughter and possessed of a generally happy disposition, Agliano was accustomed to the line at the back of his fish market, and knew most of the women by name.

Back at the front of the store, Tuto, our bolita man, stepped to the gleaming counter where yellowtail, redfish, snapper, and grouper lay next to huge lobsters, king crabs, and shrimp on mounds of cracked ice. He removed his white Borsalino, carefully running his manicured hand down the crease, and straightened his tie. Tuto was one of the best-dressed *boliteros* in Ybor City.

"*Minche,* you look like George Raft," said Agliano respectfully, always happy to see the most respected tough guy in his store. "What do you want, Tuto? Lobster, the biggest ones? Shrimp, the fat ones?"

Tuto laughed because he knew Agliano was pulling his leg. Tuto had ordered the biggest red snapper in all the catch. He had big, important people coming to eat with his family on Nochebuena, and no one could fix red snapper like his wife.

"Give me the red snapper, Agliano, or I'll blow the front off your store." Tuto liked to try and sound like the tough guys in the movies. The entire store broke out in an appreciative laugh, with Agliano laughing the loudest of all.

"The first truck came in, but the red snapper is just average. I wouldn't insult you. Can you come back at ten?"

"Ten? Come on, Agliano . . . I'm a busy man."

"Go to the Columbia and get some *café con leche* and that good toasted Cuban bread." Agliano walked him to the door.

"Ten?" Tuto wanted confirmation.

"Ma shuse, boss," Agliano imitated Henry Armetta in the movies, wiped his hands on his apron, and shook Tuto's hand.

Tuto smelled his hand and made a face. "Now I smell like a fish."

"What do you 'spect you smell like, if you shake a fishmonger's hand? A lilac?"

The morning passed in a frenzy. In the front of the store they were racking up sales and seafood was flying out the door. More people stood in line outside.

Meanwhile, the line in the back moved slowly forward. Every so often Agliano would appear with a tray of fish heads, backbones, fins, and other scraps, which would soon be simmering in pots of depression chowder all over the Bataclan, Ybor City's poor section.

Sebastiano Agliano ordered an empty fifty-gallon drum to be rolled into the yard. Filling it with wrapping paper and wooden slats from the crates, he made a big bonfire so that the ladies and the kids waiting at the back of the store would be warm. Sebastiano looked at the last woman in line. He knew her. A widow of a worker killed on the docks. She'd been waiting all night, and her two kids looked tired and unhappy. Well, he thought, I hope there is something left over for her.

Ten o'clock came around and Tuto stood at the front window on Seventh Avenue knocking on the window with his ring. He looked like he was in a big hurry. He pantomimed, looking dramatically at his fancy Gruen wristwatch, pointed to it, and raised his eyebrows.

Sebastiano checked the back of the store. No trucks had come. No red snapper. He pantomimed the hour of twelve. At twelve the biggest red snapper in the entire world would be there for Tuto. So Tuto smiled and

Sebastiano Agliano and a red snapper.

waved and he was off in his big black Buick sedan to attend to his collections. At the back of the store, the line of women steadily diminished. Still the hollow-eyed widow with her two children hung on doggedly at the back of the line.

At twelve o'clock a truck pulled up which held a truly exceptional red snapper. Sebastiano put it on ice himself, with a crudely lettered sign that read "Sold." But Tuto did not show up. One o'clock, and Tuto had still not appeared. By two o'clock the stock of fish was almost exhausted, the large showcase empty, save for Tuto's red snapper.

On Christmas Eve, it was Sebastiano's habit to close the store early so his workers could go home early and help in the preparation for the Nochebuena feast. By three o'clock they were getting restless, and Sebastiano let them go but stayed on in the store himself, the lights on, the front door open, awaiting the arrival of Tuto. Sebastiano Agliano was a man who took great pride in his work, and he looked forward to seeing Tuto's face when he beheld the giant red snapper that Sebastiano had saved for him.

Behind the store, the line had all but disappeared. Only the widow and her two children still huddled around the fifty-gallon drum, trying to stay warm, although the fire inside the drum was dying as fast as her hopes to get enough fish scraps with which to make a Nochebuena chowder. Nothing was happening inside Agliano's Fish Market. No more sales. No more fish. Still she stayed, hoping against hope that Sebastiano Agliano would find a scrap or two for her children before he closed.

By four o'clock Sebastiano had run out of things to do in the empty store and faced a tough decision. His own family was waiting for him to bring home fish for their dinner, but still he felt the obligation to wait for Tuto, Agliano's Fish Market's best customer.

At five minutes past the hour, Pepe, the town gossip, stuck his head in the door. Sebastiano was happy to see him, for he was always good for a laugh.

"Hey, Sebastiano, are you waiting for Tuto?"

"Yes, he's got the mother of all red snapper on ice. Soon as he comes I'm out of here."

"Well, you better take the fish home, because Tuto ain't coming."

"Ain't coming? Why?" He'd waited all this time, and Tuto wasn't coming? His Sicilian temper started to get the best of him. "Ain't coming! That *strunzo!*" he bellowed.

"Ain't coming now, ain't coming *never!*" Pepe stood by the open door.

"Never?"

"It was on his collecting rounds—someone was waiting for him on Columbus Drive and blew his head off."

"Dead?" Sebastiano asked automatically, at the same time realizing how stupid the question was.

"As a mackerel," said Pepe, stepping out of the store, and then he was gone, part of the Christmas crowd on Seventh Avenue.

Sebastiano Agliano sat down hard on one of the chairs at the front of the store. He put his head in his hands and felt a rush of sorrow flood over him. Poor Tuto. At the height of his fame, after so much hard work, now dead. All over and he wasn't even forty years old. Better he should have stayed in Sicily, been a farmer like his family, and lived to a ripe old age. Instead he came to America, chose to live outside the law, bought himself a fine house and car, went out with beautiful ladies, and wore Hollywood movie star clothes. And now here he was dead. Wearily, Sebastiano dried his tears. He locked the front doors, turned the sign so that it read CLOSED, and stood looking at his store. The shelves and floor were clean and glistening and everything was ship shape. How hard he had worked since his arrival, from Siracusa, in 1908. How much he had sacrificed to succeed in this new country of America. He felt a pride of accomplishment. He had a secure business, he was the envy of many in Ybor City, and he had a nice safe home with a wonderful wife and children waiting to greet him on Christmas Eve.

Just as he turned to go, his eyes fell on the huge red snapper, lying atop

Agliano's Gift.

his mountain of ice, its dead eyes staring fishily up at Sebastiano. It was at that precise moment that Sebastiano Agliano had an epiphany. That kingly red snapper, rightful property of Tuto, prince of bolita, should commemorate Tuto's passing by serving a higher purpose. Tuto had made a living by doing wrong; it was only just that his last act on that holy day of Nochebuena should be one of kindness and charity.

Taking the red snapper carefully in his hands, he placed it at the center of yesterday's *La Gaceta.* How Don Victoriano Manteiga would enjoy knowing his newspaper was a part of this wonderful gesture.

Behind the store, in the growing cold near the dying fire, the widow held on, prayer beads in her hand, her two children huddled around her. Until she saw Sebastiano's car drive off, there was hope.

And then Sebastiano Agliano himself appeared, holding the red snapper in its entirety: head, tail, and all, borne aloft on its *La Gaceta* throne as if it were the queen's crown jewels. Agliano smiled.

"Here, Maria. Your prayers are answered."

"But, how . . . ?" Maria was stunned by the magnitude of the gift. Not only would she have enough for a princely Nochebuena feast, but enough for Christmas Day and beyond. Surely this was divine intervention. Miracles happened in the blessed New World of America, but even so, this was beyond comprehension. She moved to kiss Sebastiano Agliano's hand, but he waved her off for fear of dropping the red snapper in the dirt. He finished wrapping the fish, and then, impulsively, he reached in his pocket and handed her a crisp five-dollar bill.

"Do not thank me, Maria, for this is the gift of Tuto, a man who makes his living illegally, a man who wanted to do something good on his last day on earth. Merry Christmas to you and your children, from Tuto the Bolitero."

"Merry Christmas, and thanks to Tuto," she said, still holding his gaze, "and thank you, Don Sebastiano."

Poultry and Stuffing

A turkey may be roasted stuffed or unstuffed. The stuffing may be cooked separately in a casserole or suitable baking pan. Combine ingredients just before stuffing bird. (Dry ingredients may be measured and prepared ahead of time. Liquid or moist ingredients may be measured ahead of time but must be kept in the refrigerator until they are to be combined with dry ingredients.) If one of the ingredients is meat, such as ground beef, giblets, liver, oysters, or sausage, it must be thoroughly cooked before combining it with the other ingredients. Stuff the turkey just before it is placed in the oven. Allow ¾ cup stuffing per pound of the turkey's ready-to-cook weight. If using a fresh turkey, rub ½ to 1½ teaspoons of salt, depending upon turkey size, into the cavity.

DO'S AND DON'TS FOR STUFFING POULTRY

Refrigerate the cleaned, uncooked bird and the stuffing separately in covered containers.

If you want to freeze the uncooked bird, do it with an unstuffed cavity. Freeze the stuffing in a separate container. Remember, the bird takes a long time to defrost, whereas stuffing in its own container requires much less time and should be used as soon as it has thawed.

Cook giblets in water before using in stuffing.

If meat broth is used in the stuffing, make certain the broth is well refrigerated during the period between making it and using it in the stuffing. Do not make the broth more than 24 hours before stuffing the bird.

Stuff the turkey lightly to avoid a soggy, compact stuffing.

If there is stuffing left over after the bird has been carved and served, remove the stuffing and refrigerate it separately.

Cooked stuffing should be used within 3 days and served as a leftover for one meal only.

Traditional Bread Stuffing for Turkey

4 cups day-old bread, diced
1 package prepared stuffing
1 cup diced celery
1 cup chopped onion
¾ teaspoon salt
½ teaspoon pepper

¾ teaspoon sage
1 egg, lightly beaten
¾ cup melted butter
1 cup chicken broth (see p. 38)
½ teaspoon poultry seasoning

Combine bread, stuffing, celery, onion, salt, pepper, sage, poultry seasoning, and egg. Slowly add broth and butter, tossing lightly with fork until blended. Taste; if too dry, add more broth. Stuffs a 20-lb. turkey.

Bread and Apple Stuffing for Turkey

1 medium onion, chopped
½ cup butter, melted
1 loaf fresh bread, cubed
1 teaspoon thyme

1 teaspoon sage
1 Granny Smith apple, peeled and diced
½ teaspoon salt
⅛ teaspoon black ground pepper

Sauté onion in a little butter until translucent. In a bowl, combine remaining ingredients. Add cooked onion and melted butter. For moister stuffing, add a little more butter. Stuffs a 15-lb. turkey.

Stuffed Breast of Turkey, Catalan Style

1 10½-lb. turkey
2 tablespoons extra-virgin olive oil
½ lb. mild Italian sausage,
  casing removed
½ cup pine nuts
1 Granny Smith apple, cored
  and finely chopped
½ lb. assorted dried apricots, raisins,
  and pitted prunes
2½ cups turkey or chicken broth (see
  p. 38)
½ cup dry sherry
Salt and freshly ground black
  pepper to taste

Disjoint turkey and place breast, skin side down, on a cutting board. (Freeze remaining pieces or use in other dishes.) Using a thin-bladed boning knife and keeping it close to the bone at all times, remove breastbone first and then ribs, leaving breast whole and skin intact. Lay the breast out, skin side down.

Heat 1 tablespoon oil in a medium skillet and cook sausage thoroughly over medium heat. Add pine nuts and cook until golden. Stir in apple and dried fruits; cook 2 minutes. Add sherry and ½ cup of the broth. Season lightly with salt and pepper, and cook over medium heat until the fruits have absorbed the liquid. Cool slightly for easier handling.

There will be a natural trough in middle of breast. Place filling in trough. Bring up the sides and ends to encase filling. Hold the sides together with long skewers. Sew together with string at 1-inch intervals and around from end to end, twice; then again a couple of times around to keep the two lengthwise strings in place.

Heat the remaining tablespoon of olive oil in a large pot, and carefully brown the breast all over. Add remaining 2 cups of broth and bring to a boil. Lower heat, cover, and cook 1 hour, until the internal temperature is 165 degrees. Remove breast to a cutting board and let stand 10 minutes. Skim fat from sauce; keep sauce warm. To serve, slice the breast and arrange slices on a platter, passing the sauce separately at the table. Serves 6.

Roast Chicken with Sherry

2 tablespoons extra-virgin olive oil
3–3½ lb. chicken, cut in serving pieces
Salt
Freshly ground pepper

1 tablespoon parsley, minced
2 cloves garlic, cut in several pieces
¼ cup medium-sweet sherry
2 tablespoons lard or butter

Cover bottom of a roasting pan with the oil. Arrange chicken pieces in the pan, skin side up. Sprinkle with salt, pepper, and parsley. Add garlic and pour in sherry. Dot chicken with lard or butter. Roast at 350 degrees for 50 minutes, basting frequently and adding water as the liquid evaporates. Serves 4.

Roast Turkey, Cuban Style

1 15-lb. turkey, fresh or thawed
2 teaspoons salt
2 teaspoons black pepper
1 cup sour orange juice (or ½ cup
    lemon juice mixed with ½ cup
    regular orange juice)
12 garlic cloves, finely chopped
3 lbs. ground pork
3 lbs. ground beef
6 eggs

½ cup green olives, pitted
½ cup raisins
½ cup capers
2 cups dry sherry
3 tablespoons white pepper
2 cups bread crumbs
1 cup toasted almonds, slivered

Pour citrus juice over turkey and inside cavity. Rub thoroughly inside and outside with 2 teaspoons salt, 2 teaspoons black pepper, and garlic. To make stuffing, combine remaining ingredients in large bowl.

Preheat oven to 325 degrees. Fill turkey cavity with stuffing, packing it loosely. Close cavity with trussing skewers, or sew with a trussing needle and thread. Place turkey, breast side up, on a rack in a roasting pan. Insert a meat thermometer in a thigh, being careful not to touch the bone. Put water or broth in bottom of pan, and make sure it doesn't dry up during cooking. Roast for 3½ to 4 hours, until thermometer reaches 175 degrees. (When turkey is a golden color, cover loosely with aluminum foil.) When turkey is done, place on a platter and let stand 30 minutes. Remove trussing and stuffing. Serve stuffing in a separate bowl. To make gravy, transfer pan juices to a saucepan, boil until thickened, and season with salt and pepper to taste. Serves 8–10.

Chicken in Wine Sauce

2 3½-lb. chickens, cut in 8 pieces
1½ cups extra-virgin olive oil
1 cup white cooking wine
1½ cups red wine
1 clove garlic, crushed
2 medium onions, chopped
3 cups water
1 red bell pepper, sliced
1 8-oz. can sweet peas
½ teaspoon salt
¼ teaspoon pepper
¼ teaspoon oregano
Parsley, for garnish

Put chickens in a heavy pot with salt, garlic, and oil. Sauté until golden brown. Remove hens. In same pot, add water, wine, onions, pepper, and oregano; mix well and scrape bottom of pot. Return hens to pot and cook 1 hour over very low heat. Garnish with pepper slices, peas, and parsley. Serves 6.

Roast Turkey with Mole Sauce

8–10 lb. turkey, fresh or thawed
¾ cup shelled peanuts
4 dried mulato chilies
4 dried ancho chilies
4 dried pasilla chilies
1 cup water; 4 cups water
1 teaspoon salt
⅓ cup sesame seeds;
  2 tablespoons sesame seeds
¼ teaspoon anise seeds

1 cinnamon stick
4 cloves garlic, unpeeled
¼ cup lard; 3 tablespoons lard
1 stale corn tortilla
¼ cup raisins
¼ teaspoon ground coriander
¼ teaspoon ground cloves
3½ cups turkey broth (see p. 38)
½ Mexican chocolate tablet

Preheat oven to 375 degrees. Reduce heat to 325 degrees and roast turkey unstuffed for 4–5 hours. (Or covered in aluminum foil at 450 degrees for 2¼–2½ hours.) For general instructions and reminders about roasting a turkey, see pp. 166 (Do's and Don'ts) and 169 (Roast Turkey, Cuban Style).

Toast peanuts; set aside to cool. Wash all chilies and remove seeds and stems. Place them in an ovenproof bowl with 1 cup water and steam them in the oven at 350 degrees for 15 to 20 minutes, stirring occasionally. (They can also be microwaved in a bowl with 1 cup water until they bubble, 5–8 minutes.) Remove and drain, reserving liquid.

Simmer giblets for 30 minutes over medium-low heat in 4 cups water with 1 teaspoon salt. Reserve broth.

In a skillet, toast sesame seeds over medium heat, tossing frequently until golden; remove from pan. In the same skillet toast anise seeds, cinnamon stick, and garlic over medium heat. Peel garlic and set aside.

In a blender, grind anise seeds, cinnamon, and all of the sesame seeds except 2 tablespoons. Set aside.

In a skillet, melt ¼ cup lard over medium-high heat and fry tortilla until crisp and golden. In same skillet, sauté raisins briefly, until they puff. Break tortilla in pieces, put in blender, and grind into fine crumbs. Add cooled, toasted peanuts and blend until fine. Remove mixture from blender and set aside.

Place garlic, raisins, and cinnamon-anise-sesame mixture into blender. Add coriander and cloves. Add chilies and 1 cup reserved chili liquid. Blend until smooth. Add peanut-tortilla mixture and ½ cup broth. Blend until puréed.

In a large pot, melt 3 tablespoons lard, add the blender mixture, and cook for 5 minutes, stirring constantly, over medium heat. Break chocolate into pieces and add to sauce. Lower heat and cook for 10 minutes to melt the chocolate, stirring constantly. Slowly stir in 3 cups turkey broth. Bring to a boil, lower heat, and simmer for 30 minutes.

Remove turkey from oven, cool, and slice into serving pieces. In a large casserole dish, arrange turkey pieces and pour mole (*mó-lay*) sauce over them. Heat through in a 350-degree oven, about 15 minutes. Remove from oven and sprinkle with 2 tablespoons sesame seeds. Serves 10.

Note: Mole sauce may be made up to a week in advance and kept in freezer.

Nochebuena in the Bataclan

A dear old friend, Joseph Abad, gave me his impressions and memories of Nochebuena in the Bataclan, where Ybor City's poorest families lived. His voice and the personal nature of his story so struck me that I decided to leave his reminiscence in the first person.

Just the other day I inquired of my uncle Eddy whether or not he had celebrated many Nochebuenas as a kid. "Heck, no," he said, laughing. "We were so poor that we had to come over to *your* house to celebrate after La Misa del Gallo" (Midnight Mass). Right then, I knew he was lying—about two things. First, had my uncle Eddy ever attended Midnight Mass, Our Lady of Perpetual Help herself, standing proudly next to the altar, would have exploded in shock. Second, it would have been a complete waste of time to come to *our* house for a Nochebuena handout. The sign over my dear grandmother's front door read: Brother, Can You Spare a Dime? We were so poor we didn't even have *cucarachas* (cockroaches).

But somehow, every year, someone in our huge family worked magic and came up with a few pounds of beans. One year, the local bolita operators donated a small piglet for several of the poor families in the Bataclan to share. And no matter how bad times were, we always had Cuban bread.

I cannot honestly remember ever having seen a Christmas tree in my grandmother's home. During the holidays, we never put pressure on our loving parents. Even as small children, my brothers and sisters knew and appreciated the situation our parents were in. The Abads were not unique. Some of the Bataclan families had some *really* rough Nochebuenas—in many ways we were lucky.

What was more, there was a teeny, tiny, little happy side to Nochebuena for us kids. Every year, we would all line up at Cuscaden Park to receive a wooden toy and a small bag of candy. The sponsors were the Tampa Fire Department firefighters, who made the toys themselves, and the Sportsmen's Association, God bless them. Without their big hearts, this kid, and several like me, would never have received a toy for Christmas. How strange that from all of those years, what I remember is that Santa Claus was a fireman and a bolita operator!

I remember other kids at school, after the holiday. We looked at some of them like they were nuts when they inquired if we had eaten twelve grapes on Nochebuena for good luck. Grapes! At best, we had some pecans and some Brazil nuts to eat. Forget gifts being exchanged. Forget listening to music—we had no radio or phonograph, and besides, the electricity was disconnected.

What I remember best was our family gathering around the table, everyone talking at the same time. I spent my time looking around to see who in the room was listening. The kerosene lamp gave just barely enough light to see our faces in the dark room. Even today I still remember my dear mother, with her Mona Lisa smiling face, chewing on a piece of Cuban bread. That is what I remember best about Nochebuena.

The Family Gathers around the Black-Bean Pot.

Tamales and Chili

Chicken Tamales

5 tablespoons lard

2 cups cornmeal flour (*masa harina*), or fine yellow cornmeal

1½ cups hot water or chicken broth (see p. 38)

½ teaspoon salt

1½ teaspoons baking powder

DOUGH

In a large bowl, cream lard until very light and fluffy. Sift together cornmeal, baking powder, and salt. Gradually beat flour mixture into lard. When all flour has been incorporated, add hot water or broth a little at a time, beating constantly, to form a soft dough, or *masa*.

FILLING

¾ pound cooked chicken, finely diced   6 tablespoons red chili sauce (see p. 92)

Combine chicken with chili sauce.

MAKING THE TAMALES

24 corn husks or tamale wrappers (parchment or foil)

If corn husks are being used, soak them in hot water for about ½ hour to soften; pat dry. Place a rounded tablespoonful of dough in the middle of each corn husk or tamale wrapper. Spread it into a rectangle so that it extends almost the full width but only about 3 inches along the length.

Put a rounded tablespoonful of filling on the center of each piece of dough. Fold one long side of the wrapper just past the center of the filling. Fold the wrapper on the opposite side to make an overlapping center seam. Turn the ends in over the seam, lapping them just enough to tuck one into the other. Tie a string around each tamale, like a package.

Place tamales, seam side down, in a steamer or colander, in as many layers as necessary. Steam, tightly covered, over boiling water for about 1 hour, until the dough is cooked. Pile wrapped tamales in a heated dish. Makes 24.

Red Chili Tamales with Pork

MEAT

4 lbs. pork butt or pork roast
2 quarts water
2 cloves garlic, whole

Cut up meat in ½-inch cubes, place in a large stockpot with garlic cloves, and cover with water. Cook over medium heat until almost tender, about 1 hour. Remove garlic and discard. Drain meat, reserving broth.

CHILI SAUCE

½ cup dried chili powder or 1 cup red chili (see p. 181)
½ teaspoon powdered oregano
½ teaspoon powdered cumin
1 teaspoon salt
1 tablespoon vegetable oil
1 tablespoon flour
Broth from cooked pork

In a large bowl, mix chili powder or red chili, oregano, cumin, and salt. Add broth a little at a time to make a paste. In a large saucepan, toast flour in oil over medium heat; do not allow to burn. Add the chili mixture, along with a little more meat broth if necessary to achieve a sauce consistency. For a spicier taste, add more chili powder. Add chili mixture to meat. If too dry, add a little more broth or water; it should be like a thick sauce.

CORN HUSKS

2–3 dozen corn husks

Wash husks in hot water, removing corn silks, and soak husks for ½ hour while you make the tamale dough, or *masa*. Stand them up to drain (but do not allow them to dry out).

DOUGH

2 cups lard or other solid shortening
5–6 cups fine cornmeal
2 teaspoons salt
Broth from cooked pork

In a large bowl, cream lard until light and fluffy. Add cornmeal and salt gradually, then add broth a little at a time, starting with ¼ cup, beating constantly. If too dry, add water. Dough should be spreading consistency, and it should be shiny, not dry.

MAKING THE TAMALES

Make a 3-inch ball of dough for each corn husk. (Two small husks can be used together by overlapping.) Flatten the ball into a 4-inch square in the center of the husk (bigger for a large husk, smaller for a small husk); the back of a tablespoon is an effective spreader. The square should be about ¼ to ½ inch thick. Place 2–3 tablespoons of chili-meat mixture onto center of dough square. Roll edges of husk together lengthwise, being careful not to squeeze. Tie each end with a strip from the husk (like a party favor).

STEAMING THE TAMALES

Pour 2 cups of water into a large pot with a steaming rack. Tamales should not touch bottom of pan. Make a layer of tamales across the steaming rack, then carefully stand the remainder of the tamales upright, closely packed. Steam over medium heat for 1 hour, until dough is cooked. Make sure there is sufficient water on bottom of pan so tamales do not burn. For each dozen tamales, allow an hour of cooking time. Makes 2–3 dozen. Allow 2 tamales per person.

Red Chili

20 red chili pepper pods, dried	Oil for frying
6 cups water	Salt to taste
2 lbs. boneless pork (butt or shoulder)	⅛ teaspoon cumin
4 cloves garlic, crushed	

Wash chilies and remove seeds and stems. Put water and chili pods in a large pot, and bring to a boil. Lower heat and simmer until pods are soft. Remove in batches and place in blender along with ½ cup of the chili water. Purée until thick. Put through a strainer to eliminate skins and any remaining seeds. Repeat until all chilies have been blended and strained. Mixture should be quite thick.

Chop pork in ½-inch cubes. Fry in a small amount of oil (enough to keep meat from sticking) in a large skillet, until brown. Add garlic and chili purée. Salt to taste. Simmer ½ to ¾ hour. Add cumin and simmer a bit longer. Makes 3–4 cups.

Green Chili

2 lbs. pork	2 cloves garlic, crushed
Oil for frying	8 green chilies (fresh or canned),
1 14-oz. can tomatoes	roasted, peeled, and finely chopped
(including liquid), crushed	½ teaspoon salt
	4 jalapeño peppers, chopped

Cut up pork in ½-inch cubes. Fry in small amount of oil (enough to keep it from sticking) in a large skillet. Add tomatoes, jalapeños, garlic, and chilies. Add salt. Simmer about ½ hour, seasoning to taste. If chili is too hot, add more tomatoes. Makes 5–6 cups.

Cheese and Green Chili Casserole

¼ lb. Monterey Jack cheese, grated
¼ lb. longhorn cheese, grated
6 green chilies, peeled and chopped
4 jalapeño peppers, roasted and chopped

1 green bell pepper, chopped
2 eggs, separated
1 cup milk
Butter

In a 1-qt. buttered casserole dish, place a layer of cheeses and then a layer of peppers (some of each kind). Repeat layers, ending with cheese. In a bowl, beat egg whites until stiff. Beat egg yolks separately, and add milk. Mix with whites and pour over cheese in casserole dish. Dot with butter and bake at 325 degrees for 1 hour, until mixture bubbles and cheese is melted through. Serves 4.

Note: This recipe can also be made in a square baking pan or dish, cooled, and cut in small squares to be served as an appetizer.

Stacked Enchiladas

2 corn tortillas
½ cup red chili
2 teaspoons grated longhorn cheese

2 teaspoons onion, chopped
1 fried egg (optional)
Oil for frying

In a skillet over high heat, fry tortillas in about ¼ inch oil until hot bubbles form, about 2–3 seconds on each side. Cover 1 tortilla with chili, cheese, and onion. Repeat layers. Cover with red chili and, if desired, a fried egg on top. Serves 1.

Jack Espinosa's Grandma's Nochebuena Ride

Jackie Espinosa is, by universal opinion, the funniest man ever to come out of Ybor City. His stories are legendary. Turning down a career in show business in Cuba, he chose to live in Ybor City. A teacher for many years, Jack eventually became a public information officer for the Tampa Sheriff's Department. With a great sense of the ridiculous, a wonderful way with words, and an abiding love for the foibles and idiosyncrasies of Tampa's latinos, Jack brings a storyteller's gifts to bear on the following, one of my favorite Nochebuena stories.

Nochebuena at 1611 11th Avenue in Ybor City was the best night of the year. A leg of pork that had received the proper Cuban benediction (having been marinated three days in garlic, sour orange juice, and salt) was nestled in a large pot sitting on two low-flaming burners atop a kerosene stove. My mother had begun cooking at 6:00 A.M., following orders dictated by the loving and beautiful household tyrant, Carmen Rosa Espinosa Muñoz y Ballesteros—my grandmother, Abuelita.

From her bed, this mother of my father dictated all matters relating to the dinner. She was partially paralyzed from a stroke that had completely taken all of the feeling from her right side, leaving her right hand disfigured and claw-like. Her right leg was twisted in such a way that walking was impossible. For fourteen years, my *abuela* imprisoned herself in her upstairs bedroom, too proud to let anyone but family look upon her. Only on Nochebuena did she allow herself to leave her room. My mother would dress her up in a white gown, and my cantankerous grandfather, José, placed her in a wheelchair, which was made of a regular chair nailed to a square of two-by-fours. Four Union skates bolted to the wood served for wheels. Upon this throne, my grandmother was wheeled into the dining room where the table had been set in accordance with her edict. Her annual pilgrimage was very special.

There were other things to be cooked, but with only three burners, the pig took priority. Garbanzo soup, black beans, and white rice awaited their fire. The salad of lettuce, tomatoes, and *berro* (watercress) was the last thing to be prepared.

I knew nothing of it at age five, but later I realized that we were middle-class poor: better off than some and worse off than others.

It was an interesting admixture, my family. Three stepbrothers—two Carrenos from my mother's first marriage, and one Espinosa from my father's first. I was the baby. My mother was Cuban-born of Asturian and Irish parents, while Papa's parents were from Cádiz, Spain. No one spoke about my father's real father. Mama whispered to me once that he reputedly drank much wine, played the guitar, and visited "bad women." It was Papa's stepfather, José Rosa, who lived with us on 11th Avenue. José was Asturian with very fixed ideas on all matters. Those ideas were lodged within a very hard, round, bald head. His (and my father's) stubbornness was responsible for our relative poverty. Convinced that the Crash of 1929 was not for real, they refused to stand in line at the Broadway Bank and consequently lost my grandmother's eight thousand dollars.

That Nochebuena, in addition to my parents, siblings, and grandparents at the house, there were also two police dogs and one goat. The dogs, Jackie and Nellie, belonged to my oldest brother. My brother's future father-in-law had taken a liking to me and, feeling sorry for me because I didn't have a dog of my own, he gave me the nanny goat. That took some getting used to, but the two dogs got along fine with the goat, so long as it stayed outside in the backyard.

El Visco, my father's best friend, was also in attendance. El Visco was the ugliest man I'd ever seen. His eyes were crossed, his mouth twisted to the right side, and, as if to insure that no one could ignore his calamitous countenance, he defiantly topped all of that with a monstrous black Mongolian mustache that marched downward from his nostrils on both sides of his face to his thin lower jaw.

Visco was sitting in a chair against the back wall, waiting patiently for the Nochebuena festivities to begin. Suddenly, there was a thunderously loud noise as my goat butted its way through the screen door. Visco, trying desperately to focus his crossed eyes on the goat, was toppled off his chair almost at once, his hands reaching for the hard-charging Nanny.

Alerted to the invasion of their turf by Visco's shouts, the two dogs raced in to challenge the invader. Not about to be done in, Nanny warded them off with vicious butting and bleating of a high order. Barking, howling, growling, bleating, yelling, screams—all of this noise filled every small room in our house.

Relative after relative dived at the goat, trying to catch it, and missed. The floor was littered with at least ten fallen relatives when my grandmother, making ready for her entrance, reached the top of the stairs. Planks had been set down so that she would have a smooth descent. Because of the

The Cornered Goat and the Flying Abuela.

melee below, however, Abuelita had been left alone at the top of the stairs in her wheelchair.

The goat charged again. Visco was down, Papa was down, and Mama was positioned so as to meet the charge with her wooden cooking spoon. My brothers tried with little success to rally the cowed dogs. The goat was clearly winning the day, hands down, when something happened that stopped the fray. Down the planks came the old lady in the wheelchair, mouth open, shawl flying, and picking up speed as she went. She hit the floor and never stopped until she hit the front wall with a sickening thud.

In later years, my mother speculated that if the front door had been open, my grandmother would have gone down the street like the 12th Avenue trolley, winding up at the Fourth of July Café for her Nochebuena supper.

My grandmother remained silent, smack up against the wall, a knot growing on her forehead. She seized the large bell she always carried to call for service and clanged it loudly.

Grandfathter José approached cautiously and solicitously. "Te lastimaste, vieja?" (Did you hurt yourself, old lady?") Abuelita brought the big bell down swiftly, striking the cringing José hard on the noggin! The sound it made was oddly in keeping with the Christmas feeling of Nochebuena.

"Tu madre, viejo cabrón!" (Your mama, you old goat!) she cried.

That was a Nochebuena I'll never forget. The food was served in virtual silence. Holding an ice bag to his head, José whimpered now and then.

Finally, and with a twinkle in her eye, my grandmother spoke: "Next year, instead of pig, I think we'll have goat for Nochebuena."

Then everyone laughed and began talking at the same time, reliving the battle of the goat, which had never been caught and was even then busy eating the Christmas tree.

Vegetables

Candied Sweet Potatoes

6 sweet potatoes, peeled
Water to cover
½ cup walnuts
1 cup brown sugar

1 6½-oz. can crushed pineapple (in pineapple juice), drained
¼ cup (½ stick) butter
½ cup maple syrup
Marshmallows, for topping

In a large pot, boil sweet potatoes in water for 30 minutes, or until tender. Slice in rounds and put in a buttered casserole dish. Layer with walnuts, brown sugar, pineapple, and butter. Pour maple syrup on top. Bake at 350 degrees for 20 minutes. Remove from oven and top with marshmallows. Return to oven and bake until marshmallows are brown. Serves 6–8.

Baked Eggplant Rollatini

2 eggplants, thinly sliced
2 tablespoons salt; ½ teaspoon salt
2 zucchini, diced
1½ cups mozzarella cheese, grated; 6 thin slices mozzarella

1 cup ricotta cheese
⅛ teaspoon pepper
1 16-oz. jar marinara sauce (or use homemade—see pp. 90, 91)

Place eggplant slices on a baking sheet and sprinkle with 2 tablespoons salt. Let stand 1½ hours. Blot eggplant with paper towels to remove salt and moisture. Place on a lightly oiled baking sheet and bake at 350 degrees for 15 to 20 minutes, until tender. (May also be grilled until tender.)

In a bowl, toss zucchini, grated mozzarella, ricotta, ½ teaspoon salt, and pepper. Place 2 tablespoons of mixture on each piece of eggplant. Roll up eggplant slices. Bake 30 minutes at 350 degrees. Immediately after removing from oven, place slices of mozzarella on eggplant rolls and top with marinara sauce. Serves 6.

Stuffed Eggplant

1 large eggplant
2 tablespoons shallots, chopped
½ cup cooked shrimp, chopped
½ cup crabmeat
1 egg, lightly beaten
Salt and pepper to taste

1 teaspoon parsley, chopped
1 tablespoon capers
½ cup bread crumbs
4 tablespoons butter
½ cup Parmesan or Romano cheese, grated

Cut eggplant lengthwise and bake in oven at 400 degrees, until tender. Scoop out pulp and set aside with eggplant halves. In a skillet, brown shallots in butter. Add eggplant pulp, shrimp, crabmeat, egg, parsley, salt, pepper, and capers. Mix well. Stuff eggplant halves with mixture and sprinkle with bread crumbs and cheese. Bake in 350-degree oven 15 to 20 minutes, until brown. Serves 2.

Baked Red Cabbage and Apples

2 tablespoons lard, melted,
  or extra-virgin olive oil
1 medium onion, finely chopped
1 lb. red cabbage (tough outer leaves
  removed), coarsely chopped
1 large apple, peeled, cored,
  and cut in ½-inch pieces
¼-lb. slab bacon, diced
2 tablespoons red wine vinegar

1 bay leaf
Salt
Freshly ground pepper
1 tablespoon parsley, minced
½ cup warm water
2 medium potatoes, cooked
  and diced (optional)

In an ovenproof casserole dish, melt lard or olive oil. Sauté onion over medium heat until wilted. Stir in cabbage, apple, and bacon, and cook 1 minute. Add vinegar, bay leaf, salt, pepper, parsley, and warm water. Bring to a boil, cover, and bake in a 325-degree oven for 45 minutes. Add potatoes, if desired, and bake 10 minutes more. Serves 4–6.

Greens and Potato Casserole

1 cup extra-virgin olive oil, or a mixture of olive and vegetable oil, for frying; 3 tablespoons extra-virgin olive oil
3 medium potatoes, peeled, sliced ⅛ inch thick
1 large onion, half of it thinly sliced, half chopped
Salt
2 cloves garlic, crushed
1 tablespoon parsley, minced
Freshly ground pepper
Dash paprika
3 eggs, lightly beaten
1¼ lbs. trimmed collard greens or Swiss chard, thick stems removed

Heat oil in a skillet. Add potatoes and onion slices (gradually, to prevent sticking), alternating in layers. Salt each layer lightly. Cook over medium heat, uncovered, until potatoes are just tender; lift and turn them occasionally. (The potatoes should remain separated, not in a "cake," and should not brown.)

Meanwhile, place greens in boiling water to cover, for 5 minutes. Drain. Cover with water again, adding salt to taste and 1 tablespoon olive oil. Return to a boil, cover, and cook 10 minutes more, until just tender. Drain and chop coarsely.

In a skillet, heat remaining 2 tablespoons of olive oil. Sauté chopped onion until wilted. Add greens and sauté 5 minutes. Add garlic, parsley, salt, pepper, 1 tablespoon warm water, and paprika. When potatoes are done, drain. Mix gently with greens. (The potatoes will break up a bit in stirring.) Transfer mixture to a shallow casserole dish, preferably Spanish earthenware. Pour eggs on top. Place under a broiler about 5 minutes, until eggs have formed a golden crust. Serves 4–6.

Fried Green Plantains

2 green plantains
½ cup vegetable oil
Salt to taste

Soak plantains in cold water briefly, then peel. Cut fruit into slices about 1 inch thick. Fry in oil over low heat until soft. Remove plantains and flatten to ½ inch thick by pressing between two pieces of clean brown paper. Fry again until crispy. Sprinkle with salt to taste. Serves 2.

Fried Ripe Plantains

2 ripe plantains (partially black or all black)
½ cup vegetable oil

Peel plantains and slice into rounds about ½ inch thick, at a slant. Heat oil in a skillet (oil should cover half the thickness of the plantains). Cook 10 to 15 minutes to soften, turning plantains as they brown. Fry until golden brown on each side. Using a slotted spoon, remove from skillet and drain on paper towel. Serves 2.

Yucca Fritters

2½ lbs. yucca, fresh or frozen
1 teaspoon salt
3 eggs, separated

½ teaspoon anise seeds
2 tablespoons sugar
Vegetable oil for frying

Boil yucca in a pot of water until tender. Drain, add ½ teaspoon salt, and mash until smooth (like mashed potatoes). Add beaten egg yolks, anise seeds, ½ teaspoon salt, and sugar. Beat egg whites until stiff peaks form. Fold into yucca mixture. In a large skillet, heat oil on high. Drop in mixture by tablespoonfuls. When brown, turn and brown on other side. Drain on paper towels. Fritters may be served with warm syrup, or dusted with confectioner's sugar. Serves 4.

Cabbage with Green Chili

1 head cabbage, chopped
4 slices bacon
1 jalapeño pepper, chopped

4 green chilies, chopped
¼ cup water

In a skillet, fry bacon over medium-high heat, until crisp. Remove bacon (but not grease) from pan and set aside. Reduce heat to low and add cabbage, jalapeño, green chilies, and water. Cover and steam over low heat until cabbage is tender. Add bacon and simmer 5 minutes more. Serves 4.

Squash, Corn, and Peppers Casserole

3 zucchini, finely chopped
2 large onions, finely chopped
4 jalapeño peppers, finely chopped
¼ cup chicken broth, homemade
  (see p. 38) or canned
1 16-oz. package frozen corn, or
  2 cups fresh corn scraped off cob

3 yellow-neck squash, finely
  chopped
4 green chilies, or 1 green and 1 red
  bell pepper
½ cup water

Put all ingredients in a medium pot, cover, and cook over low heat until
vegetables are tender. Serves 4.

Natalie's Latkes
(Potato Pancakes)

4 medium Idaho or Yukon Gold
  potatoes, peeled
1 large onion, quartered
2 eggs
¾ teaspoon salt
⅛ teaspoon pepper

Vegetable oil for frying
⅓ cup all-purpose flour
1 teaspoon baking powder
Applesauce or sour cream

Grate potatoes in food processor. Transfer to colander and rinse with cold
water. Wrap in towel, gently press out moisture, and set aside.

Place onion in food processor and, using a steel blade, chop finely, 10 to
15 seconds. Scrape down sides of processor bowl and add eggs, salt, pepper,
baking powder, and flour. Process 5 seconds. Add grated potatoes to bowl
and process all ingredients 5 to 10 seconds, pulsing several times.

Heat oil in a skillet, about ½ inch deep. Drop in large spoonfuls of potato
mixture and flatten slightly to make pancakes. Brown on both sides over
medium heat and drain on paper towels. Best served hot with applesauce or
sour cream. Makes 12 latkes.

Note: To reheat, place latkes in single layer on a foil-lined cookie sheet
and bake, uncovered, at 450 degrees for 7 to 8 minutes. Can be frozen.

Frances's Latkes

Vegetable oil for frying
5 lbs. medium potatoes, peeled
5 medium onions, chopped
1 cup matzoh meal
5 eggs

2 tablespoons salt
⅛ teaspoon pepper
1 cup all-purpose flour
1 vitamin C tablet

Grate potatoes and squeeze out excess moisture. Mix well with onions, matzoh meal, flour, eggs, salt, and pepper. (If batter gets brown or dark, put 1 dissolved vitamin C tablet into potatoes before you add eggs.) Heat ½ inch of vegetable oil in a skillet over medium-high heat. Make each pancake of about 2 rounded tablespoons of potato mixture; don't crowd them in skillet. Brown on each side until crispy. Makes 24 latkes.

Walnut Latkes

1 cup walnuts, halved
2½ cups mashed Idaho potatoes
2 eggs

¾ teaspoon salt
⅛ teaspoon pepper
Vegetable oil for frying

Putting aside ¼ cup walnuts for garnish, chop the rest. Prepare 2½ cups mashed potatoes according to your favorite recipe. Place in a bowl and mix with chopped nuts. Beat in eggs, salt, and pepper. In a skillet, heat oil and drop in large spoonfuls of mixture and flatten slightly to make pancakes. Brown on both sides. Garnish with walnut halves. Serves 4.

Zucchini Pancakes

2 small zucchini, sliced
3 tablespoons cottage cheese
Kosher salt and pepper to taste

1 egg
3 tablespoons matzoh meal
Vegetable oil for frying

In a small pot of water over medium heat, boil zucchini for 10 minutes. Drain. Mash zucchini and mix in cottage cheese, salt, pepper, egg, and matzoh meal. Heat about ½ inch of oil in a skillet and drop in large spoonfuls of mixture. Brown on both sides over medium heat. Serves 4.

Stuffed Cabbage

2½ lbs. ground beef
1 cup cooked white rice
1 onion, grated
1 egg
1 slice of white bread, soaked and
  torn in small pieces in water
Salt to taste

2 medium heads of cabbage
1 14-oz. can tomato purée
1 6-oz. can tomato paste or tomato
  sauce
Juice of ½ lemon
1 cup brown sugar

Core the cabbages and place in a large pot. Pour boiling water over cabbage to blanch. Separate the leaves and drain in a colander. Cut off some of the hard strip over the center of the leaves without cutting through them. In a large bowl, combine ground beef, rice, onion, egg, bread, and salt. Fill each cabbage leaf with about 2 tablespoons of the mixture, roll up, and tuck ends under. Carefully place one by one in a large pot. Mix tomato paste, tomato purée, lemon juice, and brown sugar, and pour over cabbage leaves. If there is any leftover cabbage, cut it into small pieces and add to pot.

Cook stuffed cabbage leaves either on top of the stove or in the oven. For stovetop, put pot over low heat and simmer for 2 hours. For the oven, bake at 375 degrees, covered, for 1 hour; then uncovered for 2 hours. Taste along the way and add more brown sugar if needed. Serves 4–6.

Cauliflower Soufflé

4 tablespoons butter
4 tablespoons all-purpose flour
¼ teaspoon kosher salt
¼ teaspoon dry mustard
¼ teaspoon fresh nutmeg, grated

2 cups light cream
½ cup American or cheddar cheese, grated (kosher)
4 eggs, separated, room temperature
1 small head cauliflower, cut into florets and parboiled

Melt butter in a saucepan over medium heat. Blend in flour, salt, mustard, and nutmeg, making sure the mixture does not burn. Gradually add cream, stirring constantly over low heat until it thickens. Stir in cheese until melted. Beat egg yolks in a bowl and add very slowly to cheese mixture, stirring constantly to prevent curdling. Let cool. Add cauliflower to mixture.

Butter a 1½-quart soufflé dish. Use a piece of string to tie waxed paper around the outside of the dish 3 inches higher than the lip, to extend the height of the dish. In a bowl, beat egg whites until stiff, but not dry. Fold into cheese mixture in saucepan. Pour into soufflé dish. Preheat oven to 375 degrees. Set dish in a pan of water and bake for 1 hour, or until puffed, set, and browned on top. Serves 6.

Vegetarian Cutlet

1 onion, finely chopped
½ cup celery, finely chopped
1 cup grated carrot
4 tablespoons vegetable oil; plus
  vegetable oil for frying
½ cup cooked green beans, chopped
½ cup cooked green beans, mashed

2 eggs, lightly beaten; 1 egg, lightly
  beaten with 1 teaspoon water
½ teaspoon kosher salt
⅛ teaspoon freshly ground pepper
5 tablespoons matzoh meal
½ teaspoon sugar (optional)
2 tablespoons parsley, chopped

Sauté onion, celery, and carrot in 4 tablespoons oil until tender. Let cool.
Add beans, eggs, salt, pepper, matzoh meal, and, if desired, sugar and/or
parsley. Mix well. Shape into 6 cutlets and dip each in egg beaten with water.
Heat ¼ to ½ inch of oil in a skillet over medium heat. Brown cutlets on both
sides. Serves 6.

Sweet Potato Kugel

2 cups raw sweet potatoes,
  washed, peeled, and grated
2 tablespoons vegetable oil
½ cup dark brown sugar, firmly packed
½ cup corn syrup
1 cup water
2 eggs, well beaten

¼ teaspoon kosher salt
⅛ teaspoon freshly ground pepper
Rind of ½ orange, grated
⅛ teaspoon ginger, ground
⅛ teaspoon nutmeg, ground
¼ teaspoon cinnamon, ground

In a large bowl, combine all ingredients. Pour into a greased 1-quart baking
dish. Bake uncovered at 350 degrees. When a crust begins to form, stir well.
Bake for a total of 40 minutes, stirring every 10 minutes. Excellent served
either hot with meat or cold as a dessert. Serves 5.

Carrot Tzimmes

2 cups orange juice
1 lb. carrots, peeled and sliced
½ cup dried prunes
2 tablespoons honey

In a large saucepan, warm 1 cup orange juice on low heat. Add carrots. Cook, covered, over medium-low heat for ½ hour. Add dried prunes and rest of orange juice. Cook an additional ½ hour. Turn off heat and mix in honey. Transfer to a warm plate. Serves 6.

Jellies and Relishes

Cranberry Gelatin Salad

1 cup raw cranberries, chopped
¼ cup sugar
1 orange with rind (seeds removed), chopped
1 small package raspberry gelatin
1 cup crushed pineapple in syrup
Red food coloring
1 cup celery, chopped
1 cup walnuts or pecans, chopped
½ cup hot water

Combine cranberries and sugar in food processor and chop coarsely. Let stand a few minutes. Taste and add more sugar, if desired. Add orange and chop again.

In a saucepan, dissolve gelatin in hot water. Drain pineapple and add syrup to gelatin. Let cool. Add pineapple and enough red food coloring to make it pretty. Add celery and nuts and mix well. Mixture may be poured into a mold or into a 9 x 13 inch pan. If a mold is used, grease with vegetable oil first. Chill until firm. If in pan, cut into squares. Serves 6–8.

Note: If you like firmer gelatin, use a large package with ¾ cup of hot water.

Lime Bavarian Mold

1 large package lime gelatin
1 cup hot water
1 cup orange juice
1 pint whipping cream
1 6½-oz. can crushed pineapple, drained
Maraschino cherries, for garnish

Dissolve gelatin in hot water and orange juice. When slightly jelled, beat until light and fluffy. Mix with pineapple and cream. Pour into a greased mold and chill. Garnish with maraschino cherries. For variation, add 1 cup chopped walnuts along with pineapple and cream. Serves 6.

Cranberry Relish

16 ozs. cranberries, washed
2 cups raisins
3½ cups sugar

½ cup white vinegar
1 cup pecans, chopped
½ teaspoon ground cloves

Put all ingredients in a large, heavy saucepan and bring to a boil over low heat. Simmer for 15 minutes. Use as a side dish, or place a teaspoonful inside muffins before baking. Also good on fresh or cooked pears and peaches. May be frozen, or put up in sterilized canning jars. Makes 3–4 cups.

Jalapeño Jelly

1 cup green bell peppers
  (seeds removed), finely chopped
1 cup jalapeño peppers
  (seeds removed), finely chopped
5 cups sugar

2 3-oz. pouches liquid pectin
1¼ cups apple cider vinegar
Green food coloring (optional)

In a 5-quart saucepan, mix peppers, jalapeños, sugar, and vinegar. Boil 10 minutes. Remove from heat, add pectin and food coloring, and stir vigorously. Let cool. (Stir frequently to prevent the peppers from rising to the top.) Pour jelly into sterilized canning jars. Cool and store. Makes about 4 cups.

Jalapeño Relish
(for Fire-Eaters)

4 lbs. ripe tomatoes
3 medium onions, chopped
12 jalapeño peppers
1 cup apple cider vinegar
1 teaspoon salt

½ teaspoon pepper
2 large cloves garlic, chopped
¼ cup plus 1 teaspoon sugar
1 tablespoon hot red chili powder

Drop tomatoes into a pot of boiling water for 10 seconds. Remove, cool for a few seconds, and slip off skins. Cut each tomato in half, squeeze out all juice and seeds, and chop. Using a 4-quart pot, simmer tomatoes and onions for about 10 minutes; do not overcook, or they will be mushy. Add rest of ingredients. Simmer for 20 minutes or until thick. Let cool. Put into small, sterilized canning jars. Makes 6 cups.

Hot Orange Marmalade

6 oranges, thinly sliced
3 tablespoons chili powder
3 tablespoons ground cumin
3 tablespoons ground coriander
½ teaspoon ground cloves

1½ cups orange juice
½ cup apple cider vinegar
2 tablespoons fresh jalapeño peppers,
   chopped
2 cups sugar
¼ cup molasses

Boil orange slices in hot water for 5 minutes. Remove from heat, drain, and let cool. In a large, deep saucepan over medium heat, toast the chili powder, cumin, coriander, and cloves, stirring constantly until they barely begin to smoke. Immediately add orange juice and vinegar. Stir well, adding orange slices, jalapeños, sugar, and molasses. Bring to a boil. Lower heat, simmering 45 minutes. Let cool. Put in 4- or 8-oz. sterilized canning jars. Refrigerate. Makes 6 cups.

My First Chanukah

When my family moved from Ybor City to Tampa Heights, I found a whole new world of playmates. On Columbus Drive in Ybor, almost everyone in my gang had been of Spanish descent, but in Tampa Heights, I moved in an eclectic circle of kids. Frank Spano was Italian, Henry Angulo was Cuban, and the Dawkins boys were Americans of indeterminate ancestry. Across the street lived Lionel Elozory, who was Jewish, but Lionel didn't mix much with the other kids in the neighborhood, and mostly stayed inside his big house, which also served as a boardinghouse.

Unencumbered by any notions of prejudice, I quickly made friends with Lionel and his sister Marcella. That they were Jewish meant no more to me than if they had been Mormons or Baptists—I simply never gave it a thought.

Lionel had two older sisters, Zelda and Edith, whose peculiar talent in life seemed to be to make me invisible. I don't remember that they ever addressed one word to me. Lionel's younger sister, Marcella, on the other hand, gladly played games with Lionel, my brother, and me. We spent entire afternoons on their shady front porch playing Chinese checkers, Monopoly, and Parcheesi.

Lionel Elozory in front of his dad's truck. Marcella Elozory in the back of her dad's truck.

Out in my neighborhood life, however, I lived a rowdy existence. My best pals in mischief were Byron and Marvin, the all-American Dawkins brothers. We rode our homemade scooters; played fierce games of rubber guns, hide and seek, one-two-three Klee Klee; and carried out our devilish pranks on the Tampa Electric Company streetcars. On hot summer days, the Dawkins boys and I would grease the tracks at the switch point. When the trolley started up again, its wheels would spin pointlessly, and then Byron and I would throw sandbags at the conductor, while Marvin disconnected the power cable at the back of the car. Lionel took part in none of these daredevil pastimes, for it seemed he was limited to his front steps, never going beyond them, and his only non-Jewish friend was me.

One of our favorite pastimes was to dig World War I trenches and play "All Quiet on the Western Front." In our neighborhood, as the real veterans of World War I died of the residual effects caused by the gases to which they'd been exposed in the war, their families would throw out their souvenirs. By diligent patrol of the garbage cans in the alley, we were able to come up with steel helmets, both German and American, web belts, gas masks, and so on. We dug trenches and played war in an empty lot.

By 1938 things were heating up in Europe, where Hitler was creating hell for the Jews of Germany and Austria. I read about it in *Life* magazine, but in my empty-headed way did not relate troubles in Germany to troubles in the United States.

Lionel Elozory's father ran a secondhand furniture store over on Franklin Street. The few times I was allowed in it, I was amazed and delighted. Today we would call it an antique store, for it was Mr. Elozory's habit to buy and sell the detritus of people's lives. The shop's *pièce de résistance* was an 1864 Springfield muzzle-loading rifle from the Civil War. Mr. Elozory would observe my blissful ignorance and childish joy in holding that historic gun, or watch me as I scooted along the sidewalk in front of his house wearing my prized 1914 German spike helmet, and he would shake his head.

We were all a little afraid of Mr. Elozory, who never smiled or joked or seemed friendly. The only time I can remember that he spoke much to me was one day when I appeared on his porch, ready to play games with Lionel and Marcella, who weren't home yet.

On that day, Mr. Elozory took me to what looked like a storage room and brought out a box. First he showed me a strange hat, some unidentifiable bits of uniform, and then he showed me a book full of photos of men in fez hats and uniform, some of them on camels, in the middle of the desert.

"I was in the Turkish Army." He pointed to a photograph. "We fought in the desert for two years against a man named Lawrence of Arabia. You heard of him?"

"No," I answered truthfully. Elozory sighed and closed his book. He had said enough. Now for the message.

"I see you play war games. You and the boys like the war, eh?" He put his hands on my shoulder, his eyes narrowed. "Boy, war is terrible. *Never* let them take you to war!"

With that he led me back outside. I couldn't make heads or tails of what he had said, and I never mentioned it to Lionel or Marcella.

The country was rapidly headed for war. Roosevelt had announced the Lend-Lease Act in 1941, meant to help embattled England. It was common rhetoric to argue that if your neighbor's house was burning, it made sense to lend him your fire-fighting equipment and help him put it out. So, I reasoned, if Hitler's black-shirted SS troops were coming down Lamar Street to kill the Jews, wouldn't my neighbor want me to help stop them? Sooner than I expected, I had a chance to test my reasoning.

Though I didn't know it, it was the third day of Chanukah that early December morning when I went out to get the *Tampa Tribune* for my dad. Across the street, I saw two boys with a bag of sugar sneaking furtively up to Mr. Elozory's furniture van, which was parked in front of his house. They were unscrewing the gas cap as I approached.

"What are you guys doing?" I asked, always happy to be in on a devilish prank.

"Puttin' sugar in the kike's gas tank."

"Kike?" I said, unfamiliar with the term.

The kid pointed at the menorah in the Elozorys' window. "See, he's a Jew. A kike."

"So?"

"So we put sugar in his gas, and it screws up his whole motor."

"What?" The blood rushed to my head. This was not a prank. They meant to destroy Mr. Elozory's truck. And all because he was a *Jew*? It didn't make any sense. Instinctively, I struck out at the bag. It fell, the sugar spilling on the red-bricked street. They looked at me menacingly, but they weren't any older than me, or any bigger, and there were only two of them. What was more, I was on home turf in front of my own house—all I had to do was yell for my father and *he* would take care of things. Defeated, they skulked off muttering threats and curses.

I went inside and told my father what had happened. He sighed a heavy sigh, sorry to have me introduced so young to such evil. "You did the right thing," he said, patting my head. "I'm proud of you."

"But shouldn't we tell Mr. Elozory?"

"No. Believe me, he knows about anti-Semitism. I'll take care of those two kids." My father was a man of his word, and I never saw those two again.

So it was that I was introduced to anti-Semitism with a bang, right there on Lamar Street, in front of my own house, during Chanukah.

A Gift from My Godfather, Isaac Levy

If ever I had a godfather, a real godfather who loved me, kept up with my life, rewarded my accomplishments and remembered me on holidays and birthdays, it was a dear, soft-spoken, southern Jewish man by the name of Isaac Levy.

When I was young, my father, J.B., worked for Mr. Levy at his pharmaceutical warehouse, Levy Wholesale Drugs. The big red-brick building was located on Morgan Street. I would go to Mr. Levy's office, where he would lift me onto his green blotter and talk to me in his special way about the future my father had mapped out for me. I was to become a doctor. Mr. Levy was absolutely sure I'd make it, and if Mr. Levy said so, then it must surely be so. Before I left he never failed to give me two pieces of hard candy from the jar he kept on his desk—one for immediate consumption, and one for later.

We often made family visits in those days to the beautiful Hyde Park home of Mr. and Mrs. Levy. They were childless and in a sense adopted my brother and me. The visits thrilled us. Tea and sweets were the highlight, as well as the hours we passed in grown-up chatter with Mr. Levy, who had an easy, comic way with a story and found a rapt audience in my brother and me.

The war came, we grew up, and my father opened a retail store, La Economica Drug Store, in order to make enough money to put my brother and me through medical school. We saw Mr. and Mrs. Levy less often. No more wonderful teas with strawberry jam, and no more wonderful stories.

But every year, on December 8, Mr. Levy would appear at our house on Lamar Street with a birthday present for me, and a beautiful card signed by

My godfather, Isaac Levy.

him and Mrs. Levy. The presents were always special. A silver buckle with my initials, F.P., embossed in block letters. Can anyone forget the first time they were given a truly adult and important gift? An eleven-year-old who has his own silver belt buckle embossed with his very own initials has arrived at a high social plateau he may never reach again!

Mr. Levy also appeared every Nochebuena. He dropped by to eat with us as a social courtesy—and because he loved my mother's black beans and rice. Every year he brought gifts, and again, his were always the gifts that made you feel like swaggering, that made you feel like an adult. One gift in particular I have never forgotten or lost: a red Sheaffer pen with a white dot on the cap. When he gave it to me, Mr. Levy explained that the little white dot represented the pen manufacturer's solemn promise to replace the pen, no matter if it was in pieces or wrecked beyond recognition, so long as the owner produced the white dot. Mr. Levy fixed me with a look over his rimless spectacles, and with a sly smile playing on his lips, he said, "For as long as you live, the Sheaffer Company will replace the pen, so long as you return the white dot."

I treasured my Sheaffer lifetime-guarantee red fountain pen for years, careful never to lose or damage the cap and its little white dot. That fountain pen and what it reminded me of—Mr. Levy's faith in me—saw me through my long undergraduate career, through two years of service in the Air Force, to medical school at last, just as Mr. Levy had predicted.

One night when I was a third-year medical student doing my rounds at 3:00 A.M., a man collapsed at my feet in the throes of an epileptic seizure. I rushed to his side—I was, after all, a medical student. But all I could remember to do was put something in his mouth, which was foaming up fast, to keep him from biting his tongue. Having nothing else handy, I stuck Mr. Levy's white-dotted red fountain pen into the man's mouth.

Predictably, my patient bit my pen to pieces. Frantically, I retrieved them, including, thank goodness, the white dot, my guarantee for a new pen. The man writhed on the floor, a royal blue foam bubbling from his mouth. I ran break-neck down the hall for help, rehearsing in my mind as I went a catalog of highly improbable hypotheses for the strange blue-foam phenomenon I'd just witnessed.

I considered testing the Sheaffer Company's white-dot guarantee, but felt reluctant to do so. It had been a gift from Mr. Levy and had seen me through my whole adult life up to that point. How could I, in all conscience, part with that pen? I couldn't. What's left of it sits in my safe deposit box, even now.

While still a medical school student in Miami, I came back to Tampa one summer break to work as a pharmacist and to earn extra money for tuition. What luck to find that Mr. Levy had bought the Davis Island Pharmacy and needed a temporary pharmacist for the summer.

Mr. Levy was in his eighties by then. His wife had died, and he had immersed himself in running the small drugstore. Imagine my joy at spending time with Mr. Levy again! Imagine his joy in hiring me, as he had my father, to work for him. What a wonderful summer I spent with that dear old man. I even managed finally to tell him how much he meant to me.

Mr. Levy died in his nineties, still serving the public. The picture you see included in this book is old and scratched, but if you look hard, you can see his soft face, his half-smile, and a look of love. That's the way I remember my godfather, Mr. Levy.

Desserts

Pumpkin Pie

2 eggs
¾ cup brown sugar
1 teaspoon ground cinnamon
½ teaspoon ground ginger
¼ teaspoon ground cloves

½ teaspoon salt
1¾ cups cooked or canned pumpkin
1½ cups evaporated milk
1 unbaked 9-inch pie shell

Preheat oven to 350 degrees. Beat eggs lightly in a large bowl. Combine brown sugar and spices in a small bowl. Add pumpkin and sugar-and-spice mixture to eggs. Mix well. Gradually stir in evaporated milk. Pour into pie shell. Bake in preheated oven for 40 to 50 minutes, until firm, or until knife inserted comes out clean. Serves 6.

Mincemeat Pie

2½ to 3 cups mincemeat (see below for recipe, or use readymade)
1–2 tablespoons orange juice or brandy
½ cup chopped apple (if using readymade mincemeat)
Unbaked pastry for 9-inch double crust

Mix mincemeat, apple, and orange juice or brandy. Fill pastry-lined pie pan with mixture. Cover with top crust. Bake in a preheated 450-degree oven for about 30 minutes. Serves 6.

MINCEMEAT

½ lb. fresh beef suet, finely chopped
1 16-oz. package seedless raisins
4 cups chopped apples
½ cup ground orange peel
¼ cup ground lemon peel
2 cups sugar

1 teaspoon nutmeg
1 teaspoon allspice
1 teaspoon ground cinnamon
½ teaspoon ground cloves
½ cup apple juice
½ cup brandy

In a large pot, combine all ingredients except apple juice and brandy. Mix thoroughly. Pour in 2 cups apple juice. Simmer gently over low to medium heat, stirring occasionally, for 50 minutes. Add brandy and simmer for 10 more minutes. If mincemeat is too dry, add more apple juice. Place in a large bowl. Let cool. Package in airtight containers and refrigerate 3 days. Makes about 3 quarts.

Gingerbread Cookies

½ cup butter (1 stick)
¾ cup sugar
½ cup molasses
¼ cup water
2½ cups all-purpose flour

½ teaspoon salt
½ teaspoon baking soda
1 teaspoon ground ginger
Raisins or red-hot cinnamon candies,
    for decoration

Cream butter and ½ cup sugar in a large bowl. Add molasses and water, and mix well. In another bowl, sift together 2 cups flour, salt, baking soda, and ¾ teaspoon ginger. Add gradually to molasses mixture. Roll dough into a ball. Chill in refrigerator for at least 2 hours.

Line a cookie sheet with aluminum foil. In a bowl, mix together ½ cup flour, ¼ cup sugar, and 1 teaspoon ginger. Use this mixture to flour the rolling pin and flat surface. Roll out cookies to ¼-inch thickness (thicker for larger cookies). (If desired, use a soda straw before baking to make a perfect hole in each cookie, for hanging as decorations later.) Bake cookies at 375 degrees for 10 minutes, or until golden brown. Ice cookies if desired (see below). Decorate with raisins or red hots. Makes 30 cookies.

ICING

1 tablespoon butter
1½ cups confectioners' sugar

¼ cup canned skim milk

Mix all ingredients in a bowl. For a thicker consistency, add more sugar. Spread on warm (not hot) or cool cookies.

Apple Pie

½ cup white sugar
½ cup brown sugar
1 teaspoon cinnamon

1 9-inch pie crust, unbaked
1½ tablespoons butter
6–7 cups fresh apples, peeled and cut up

Preheat oven to 425 degrees. In a bowl, mix white sugar, brown sugar, and cinnamon. Add apples and mix. Heap into pastry-lined pie pan. Dot with butter. Cover evenly with topping (see below). Bake for 50 to 60 minutes, or until crust is browned. Serves 6.

TOPPING

¾ cup all-purpose flour
½ cup sugar
⅓ cup butter, softened

In a bowl, mix all ingredients with your hands until mixture is coarse and crumbly. Set aside.

Note: This topping can be used on any fruit pie.

Pecan Pie with Rum

¼ cup butter (½ stick), melted
⅔ cup sugar
1 cup white corn syrup
3 eggs, beaten

1 teaspoon vanilla extract
¼ cup light rum
1 cup chopped pecans; 20 whole pecans
1 9-inch pie crust, unbaked

In a large mixing bowl, combine butter, sugar, corn syrup, eggs, vanilla, and rum. Beat for 3 or 4 minutes. Fold in chopped pecans. Pour into pie shell. Place whole pecans in a circular pattern on top of mixture. Bake in a 375-degree oven for 45 minutes, or until set. Serves 6.

Chewy Fruitcake Bars

2 cups Bisquick
2 tablespoons sugar
¼ cup solid butter (½ stick)
1 cup coconut, flaked

2 cups candied fruit
1 cup dates, chopped
1 cup nuts, chopped
1 15-oz. can sweetened condensed milk

Heat oven to 350 degrees. Mix Bisquick and sugar. Cut butter in thoroughly. Press mixture with floured hands in an ungreased 9 x 13 inch pan. Bake for 10 minutes. Sprinkle coconut over baked layer. Layer candied fruit and dates over coconut. Sprinkle chopped nuts over fruit. Drizzle milk on top. Bake for 25 to 30 minutes, until light golden brown. Let cool. Cut into 2 x 2 inch bars. Makes about 24 bars.

Italian Sesame Cookies

2½ cups all-purpose flour
2 teaspoons baking powder
½ teaspoon salt
1 cup sugar
1½ teaspoons cinnamon

5 tablespoons solid shortening
3 eggs, beaten
1 teaspoon vanilla extract
2 lbs. sesame seeds, lightly moistened

Sift together flour, baking powder, salt, sugar, and cinnamon. Blend in shortening. Gradually add eggs and vanilla, and knead into a ball. Roll each cookie by hand into the shape of a small cigar, 3 to 4 inches long. Then roll them in moist sesame seeds and arrange on greased baking sheet. Bake at 350 degrees for 25 to 30 minutes, or until golden brown. Makes 36–48 cookies.

Ricotta Triangles

7 cups all-purpose flour
½ teaspoon salt
1 cup solid shortening

½ cup sugar
1¼ cups lukewarm water
Vegetable oil for frying

Combine flour and salt in a large bowl. Cut in shortening. Dissolve sugar in warm water and beat into flour mixture. Knead well on a flat surface, shaping dough into a ball. Cut into quarters. Knead each piece again. Cover and set aside for 1 hour.

FILLING

3 lbs. ricotta cheese
½ cup semisweet chocolate chips
1 teaspoon cinnamon
1 teaspoon vanilla extract

½ cup sugar
Beaten egg whites
Confectioners' sugar and
    cinnamon for decoration

Combine ricotta, chocolate chips, cinnamon, vanilla, and sugar in a large bowl. Set aside. Roll each piece of dough to ⅛-inch thickness and cut into 3½-inch squares. Brush each square with egg white. Fill center with 1 tablespoon ricotta mixture and fold dough over to make a triangle. Press edges to seal and prick top with a fork. Place filled triangles on a floured cloth or waxed paper.

Heat ¼ to ½ inch of oil in a skillet over medium heat. Place triangles gently into hot oil, leaving space around them. When edges become golden, turn carefully and fry on the other side. Remove. Drain on paper towels. Sprinkle on confectioners' sugar and cinnamon. Makes about 1 dozen.

Sfingi
(Sicilian Puffs)

PASTRY

1 cup water
½ cup butter (1 stick)
1 cup all-purpose flour
⅛ teaspoon salt

4 eggs
1 tablespoon sugar
½ teaspoon grated orange peel
1 tablespoon grated lemon peel

Preheat oven to 400 degrees. In a saucepan, bring water and butter to a boil. Mix flour and salt in a bowl, and add to boiling liquid. Stir constantly, until mixture draws away from the side of the pan and is smooth and shiny. Remove from heat. Add whole eggs one at a time, beating vigorously after each addition. Mix in thoroughly the sugar, orange peel, and lemon peel.

Spoon onto a greased baking sheet, leaving a 2-inch space between pastries if using a teaspoon, a 3-inch space if using a tablespoon. Bake for 10 minutes. Reduce heat to 325 degrees and bake for an additional 30 minutes, or until golden brown. Remove puffs and let cool well before adding filling.

FILLING

1 lb. ricotta cheese
½ cup sugar
2 tablespoons chocolate chips

2 tablespoons light rum
¼ teaspoon almond extract

Mix ricotta and sugar thoroughly. Stir in chocolate chips, rum, and almond extract. Cut a slit on the side of each puff and spoon in ricotta filling. Makes 24 sfingi.

Pinulata
(Fried Sicilian Pastry)

3 tablespoons butter
3 cups all-purpose flour
6 eggs
1 cup vegetable oil

1 cup sugar
1 tablespoon grated orange peel
2 tablespoons broken pecans
1 strip lemon peel

To make the dough, cream butter into flour, adding eggs one at a time. Knead until smooth and firm, about 5 minutes. Divide into large pieces of dough and roll each into a rope about ¼ inch wide; cut into 1-inch pieces.

Heat oil in a large skillet. The oil is hot enough when you drop in a piece of dough and it floats to the top. Fry dough pieces, stirring constantly until golden brown and making sure pieces are not crowded together. Remove with a large slotted spoon and drain on paper towels.

In a saucepan over medium heat, caramelize a cup of sugar by melting it and cooking until it is until golden brown. Add orange peel and pecans. Remove lemon peel. Add 3 cups of dough pieces, stirring until each piece is coated. Remove from pan onto a dampened flat surface. With wet hands, quickly form pinulata into 3-inch clusters. Makes 8–10 pastries.

Cannoli

PASTRY

1⅔ cups all-purpose flour
½ teaspoon salt
2 tablespoons butter, chopped
1 whole egg, lightly beaten

2 egg whites, lightly beaten
¼ cup dry sherry or white wine
Vegetable oil for frying
Powdered sugar

Sift flour and salt into a bowl. Make a well in the center and put in butter and beaten whole egg. Stir with a fork, working out from the center. Add 1 egg white and sherry or white wine, a little at a time, until dough begins to stick together. Dough should be firm and somewhat dry. Shape into a ball. Cover and let stand for 15 to 20 minutes.

On a floured board, roll out dough into a circle about ⅛ inch thick. Using a sharp knife, cut into 3½-inch circles and roll these circles into ovals. Wrap each oval around a cannoli tube (available in houseware departments). Close ends and seal edges with egg white; turn out ends to flare slightly. In a deep skillet or pan, fry 2–3 pieces of dough at a time in deep hot oil for about 1 minute, or until golden brown. Remove and push each pastry gently off the form, using a fork. Let cool. Sprinkle with powdered sugar.

FILLING

4 cups ricotta cheese
1½ cups granulated sugar
½ cup finely chopped orange peel
½ cup finely chopped candied cherries
½ cup chopped semisweet chocolate
1 cup whipped cream

Press ricotta through a sieve and into a bowl. Add sugar, orange peel, cherries, and chocolate, blending well. Fold in whipped cream. Chill for 3 hours.

Using a pastry bag or a small spoon, insert filling into baked shells. Serves 8–10.

Cubiata (Italian Nougat Candy)

1 cup honey
2 egg whites
1 cup sugar
2 tablespoons water
2⅓ cups toasted hazelnuts
2 cups unblanched almonds

Heat honey in top of double boiler over boiling water, stirring with a wooden spoon. Remove pot from heat. In a bowl, beat egg whites until stiff peaks form. Add to honey, a tablespoon at a time, beating well with wooden spoon after each addition. Set aside.

Combine sugar and water in a skillet. Boil over medium heat, stirring occasionally, until caramelized. Add caramelized sugar to honey mixture by tablespoonfuls, mixing well each time. Transfer mixture to a heavy saucepan. Stirring constantly, cook over medium heat until a small amount forms a soft ball in cold water (240 degrees on a candy thermometer). Remove saucepan from heat when testing. Add hazelnuts and almonds, mixing well. Quickly divide in half and pour into two greased 8 x 8 inch cake pans. Cut nougat into 1 x 2 inch pieces and wrap in waxed paper.

Panettone Milanese (Milanese Cake)

½ package (½ tablespoon) active dried yeast	3 egg yolks
5 tablespoons lukewarm water	5 ozs. lukewarm milk
3 cups all-purpose flour	¼ cup butter, slightly softened;
⅓ cup superfine granulated sugar	1 tablespoon melted butter
¼ teaspoon salt	3 tablespoons seedless raisins
	½ cup candied citron peel, chopped

Start panettone, which is really more like a sweet bread than a cake, the day before you plan to bake it, and do not hurry the dough.

In a small bowl, sprinkle yeast over lukewarm water. Whisk well. Set aside until yeast has completely dissolved.

Sift together flour, sugar, and salt in a large, warmed bowl. Make a hollow in the center. In a separate bowl, beat egg yolks with lukewarm milk. Add yeast and egg yolk mixtures to hollow in flour, drawing in flour from the sides. Beat in ¼ cup butter, and continue beating until dough is smooth. Cover bowl with a damp cloth or a greased plastic bag, and set it to rise in a warm place until it has doubled in bulk, about 1½ hours.

Punch down the dough and, using your hands, beat it until it no longer sticks to the sides of the bowl. Cover bowl tightly with plastic wrap or foil. Refrigerate overnight.

Turn dough out onto a lightly floured surface, knead until smooth, and flatten. Scatter with raisins and chopped citron peel, and knead lightly into the dough until well distributed. Gather dough into a ball and place in an 8-inch round cake pan, well-buttered and fitted with a foil or baking parchment cuff, like a soufflé dish. Set aside to rise in a warm place, until dough has again doubled in bulk and little air bubbles begin to appear on the surface.

Preheat oven to 350 degrees. Cut a shallow cross in top of dough and brush with melted butter. Bake for about 35 minutes, or until cake is firm and has a rich, golden color. Cool on a wire rack.

Zabaglione (Egg Custard) with Strawberries

6 egg yolks
½ cup superfine granulated sugar
½ cup Marsala or other dessert wine

1 egg white
1¼ cups (10 ozs.) small
   strawberries

In the top of a double boiler, whisk together egg yolks and sugar until frothy. Stir in wine. Place over gently simmering water in double boiler. Whisk until mixture is very thick and has doubled in volume. Remove from heat and cool completely, beating constantly. In a small bowl, beat egg white until stiff. Fold into custard. Transfer zabaglione to a dish and arrange strawberries around it. Serves 4.

Sicilian Cake with Chocolate Frosting

5 x 10 inch sponge cake
  (homemade or packaged)
1 lb. ricotta cheese
6 teaspoons Strega liqueur
1 cup confectioners' sugar
¼ cup heavy cream

½ teaspoon vanilla extract
1 cup mixed candied fruit, chopped
¼ cup pine nuts
3 ozs. semisweet chocolate, coarsely
  chopped

With a very sharp serrated knife, trim ¼ inch off ends of cake; if top is rounded, level it off. Then slice cake horizontally into 3 or 4 even slices, each about ½ inch thick. Place pieces on a pastry board side by side. Sprinkle with 3 tablespoons liqueur. Set aside.

Beat ricotta and cream with an eggbeater, until very smooth. Add sugar, vanilla, and 3 tablespoons liqueur. Beat for 1 to 2 minutes. Fold in candied fruit, nuts, and chocolate.

Place bottom slice of cake on a serving platter. Spread generously with ricotta-cream filling. Place another slice of cake on top, spread with filling, and continue layering, ending with cake. Lightly press slices together, then square them neatly. Refrigerate for 3 to 4 hours, until cake feels firm to the touch. Frost (see recipe below).

CHOCOLATE FROSTING

12 ozs. semisweet chocolate chips
½ cup very strong coffee
¼ cup heavy cream

12 tablespoons unsalted butter
Candied fruit and pine nuts, for
  decoration

In a saucepan over low heat, combine chocolate chips with coffee and heavy cream, stirring constantly until chocolate has completely melted. Remove from heat.

Cut butter into small pieces and add a few at a time to the chocolate, beating into a smooth mixture after each addition. Refrigerate until mixture thickens but is still spreadable. Spread on sides and top of cake. Decorate with candied fruit and pine nuts. Cover loosely with waxed paper and refrigerate overnight. Serves 8–10.

Spumoni

½ gallon chocolate ice cream
½–¾ cup white rum, as preferred
½ gallon vanilla ice cream
1 tablespoon almond extract

1 large jar maraschino cherries,
    quartered and drained
½ gallon lime sherbet
1 bag slivered almonds, toasted

Let chocolate ice cream soften slightly in large bowl. Add rum and beat with a hand mixer just enough to mix; work fast so ice cream does not get runny. Pour into a 9 x 13 inch baking pan and freeze immediately, for at least 1 hour. (May freeze up to a day ahead.)

Prepare vanilla ice-cream layer as you did the chocolate, except add almond extract before mixing, and fold in cherries last. Spread vanilla layer over top of chocolate layer and freeze for at least 1 hour.

Work especially fast with the lime layer so that it stays very stiff. Stir a little and fold in almonds. Spread over top of vanilla layer and freeze immediately. Cut in squares. Serves 12.

Turrón
(Almond Nougat Candy)

1½ cups blanched almonds
1⅛ cups water
1⅔ cups superfine granulated
   sugar; plus extra, for dusting

4 egg yolks, beaten
Almond oil or a flavorless vegetable oil

Leave the almonds as they are or toast all or some of them. Grind at least ⅔ of them to a paste. The remainder may be ground, chopped, slivered, or left whole. Set aside almonds and almond paste.

Heat sugar and water in a heavy-bottomed saucepan. When sugar has dissolved completely, boil liquid rapidly for about 7 minutes, or until small drops harden instantly on a cold plate. Remove from heat and add almonds and almond paste, stirring until mixture forms a thick paste that leaves the sides of the pan. Stir in egg yolks.

Line a loaf pan with paper brushed with almond or vegetable oil and cut neatly to fit. Press candy evenly into pan and cover with another piece of oiled paper and a piece of heavy cardboard cut to fit. Weight the top. Let candy set in a cool place.

Turn out the candy, remove oiled paper, and dust the top with superfine granulated sugar. Use a very hot skewer to burn crisscross lines on top of the *turrón*. Cut into small squares.

Casadielles
(Walnut-Filled Turnovers)

Frozen puff pastry or homemade pie dough
1 cup ground walnuts
½ cup granulated sugar; extra, for glaze
½ teaspoon cinnamon

1 tablespoon sherry
1 tablespoon melted butter
1 egg, lightly beaten, for glaze

Prepare pastry. Mix walnuts, sugar, and cinnamon. Stir in sherry and butter. Roll pastry to ⅛ inch. Cut into 3½-inch circles. Fill each circle with 1 tablespoon walnut filling. Brush edges with water, fold over, and press with a fork to seal well. Brush with beaten egg. Bake in 400-degree oven for about 10 minutes. Sprinkle with sugar. Eat warm or at room temperature. Makes 12–14.

Torrijas
(Spanish French Toast)

1 loaf Cuban or French bread	3 eggs
1 quart milk	1 cup vegetable oil
3 ozs. dry Spanish sherry	Sherry syrup (see below)
Cinnamon	

Cut bread in 1-inch slices and trim edges. Soak bread in milk. Drain, sprinkle with sherry, and dust with cinnamon. Beat eggs until slightly foamy. Dip bread slices in egg; drain. In a skillet, fry bread on both sides in ½-inch-deep hot oil until golden. Drain and place on a platter. Pour sherry syrup over toast. Serves 6–8.

SHERRY SYRUP

½ cup water	1 strip lemon peel
1½ cups sugar	¼ cup Spanish cream sherry

Boil water, sugar, and lemon peel until sugar is well dissolved. Remove from heat. Remove lemon peel and add sherry.

Brazo Gitano
(Cream-Filled Roll)

FILLING

5 egg yolks
½ cup sugar
⅓ cup cornstarch
2 cups milk

Pinch of salt
1 cinnamon stick
1 teaspoon vanilla extract

In a heavy saucepan, beat egg yolks with a wooden spoon until lemon colored. Add sugar and beat well. In a bowl, dissolve cornstarch in a little of the milk and add to egg mixure. Then add salt, rest of milk, and cinnamon stick. Cook over medium heat, stirring constantly, until mixture thickens to a heavy custard. Remove from heat, add vanilla, and remove cinnamon stick. Set aside to cool.

SYRUP

1½ cups sugar
1 cup water

Peel of 1 lemon
½ cup dry sherry

Boil sugar, water, and lemon peel for 10 minutes. Add sherry, remove lemon peel, and set aside.

MERINGUE

5 egg whites
¼ teaspoon cream of tartar

1 cup sugar

Combine egg whites with cream of tartar and beat with electric mixer until soft peaks form. Add sugar gradually and beat until stiff.

CAKE

7 eggs, separated	1 cup cake flour, sifted
¾ cup sugar	

Beat egg whites in electric mixer at high speed until soft peaks form. Add yolks, one at a time. Add sugar, 1 tablespoon at a time. Slow mixer to folding speed and add flour gradually. Spread batter in an 11 x 16 inch jelly-roll pan lined with waxed paper. Bake at 400 degrees for 12 minutes.

Sprinkle pastry cloth or smooth-weave kitchen towel lightly with sugar. When cake is done, invert on towel and remove waxed paper. Spread cake with filling and roll up starting from one of the 11-inch sides, like a jelly roll. Place in an ovenproof serving dish. Soak cake slowly and evenly with syrup. Cover completely with meringue. Bake at 425 degrees for 6 to 8 minutes, until meringue is lightly browned. Cut cake crosswise.

Brazo Gitano de Chocolate (Chocolate Whipped-Cream Roll)

FILLING

3 egg yolks	½ cup unsweetened cocoa
¾ cup sugar	⅛ teaspoon salt
3 tablespoons cornstarch	2 teaspoons vanilla extract
3 cups milk	

In a medium-sized, heavy-bottomed saucepan, beat egg yolks with a wooden spoon until lemon colored. Add sugar and beat well. In a bowl, dissolve cornstarch in a little of the milk and add to egg mixture. Add cocoa, salt, and remainder of milk. Cook over medium heat, stirring constantly with a wire whisk until mixture thickens and boils. Boil, still stirring, for 1 minute. Remove from heat and stir in vanilla. Let cool.

SYRUP

1 cup sugar

1 cup water

½ cup coffee liqueur or chocolate liqueur

Boil sugar and water until sugar dissolves. Add liqueur. Set aside.

CAKE

3 tablespoons cake flour

4 tablespoons unsweetened cocoa

7 eggs, separated

7 tablespoons sugar

Sift flour and cocoa together into a bowl. Beat egg whites and sugar in an electric mixer at high speed until stiff, adding egg yolks gradually. Lower speed, add flour and cocoa mixture, and blend well. Spread batter in an 11 x 16 inch jellyroll pan lined with waxed paper. Bake at 400 degrees for 8 to 10 minutes.

Sprinkle a pastry cloth or smooth-weave kitchen towel with sugar. When cake is done, immediately invert on towel and remove waxed paper. Spread cake with filling and roll up from one of the 11-inch sides, like a jelly roll. Place on a serving dish and pour syrup (see above) evenly over cake. Let cool. Frost with icing (see below). Cut crosswise.

ICING

5 ozs. unsweetened baking chocolate, melted

3 cups sifted confectioners' sugar

6 tablespoons butter, softened

1 egg

½ cup milk

2 teaspoons vanilla extract

Combine all ingredients in a mixing bowl. Set bowl in a larger bowl containing ice cubes. Beat mixture until it reaches spreading consistency.

Flan
(Spanish Custard)

1 cup sugar
1 14-oz. can sweetened condensed milk
1 12 oz. can evaporated milk

1 teaspoon vanilla extract
3 whole eggs
2 egg yolks

Caramelize sugar in a baking pan or dish (9½ x 5½ x 2½ inches), cooking on stovetop over low heat, stirring frequently, until golden brown. Mix rest of ingredients in a blender at medium speed. Pour this mixture over sugar in baking pan. Place pan in a larger water-filled pan and bake in a preheated oven at 350 degrees for 1 hour. (Do not let water boil or custard will be filled with holes.) Let cool. Use a knife to loosen edges of custard from sides of pan. Turn flan upside down on a large plate. Serves 6–8.

Crema Catalana
(Catalan Cream Custard)

4 egg yolks
½ cup sugar
¼ cup cornstarch
2 cups milk
½ teaspoon salt

1 strip lemon peel
1 strip orange peel
1 cinnamon stick
1 tablespoon vanilla extract

Beat yolks lightly in a stainless steel or nonstick saucepan. Add sugar; beat well with wire whisk. Add cornstarch and milk; mix thoroughly. Add salt, lemon peel, orange peel, and cinnamon stick. Blend well and cook over medium heat, stirring constantly. When custard thickens, cool for 1 minute, stirring. Remove from heat. Remove lemon and orange peel and add vanilla. Let cool. If desired, custard may be put in individual heatproof ramekins, sprinkled with sugar, and placed directly under broiler until sugar caramelizes. Serves 4–6.

Polvorones
(Powdered Cookies)

1 cup solid shortening
1 cup plus 2 tablespoons sugar
2 eggs
4 cups all-purpose flour

½ teaspoon baking powder
¼ teaspoon salt
1 tablespoon Spanish brandy
Confectioners' sugar

In a large bowl, cream shortening and sugar, adding eggs one at a time. Sift flour, baking powder, and salt into mixture in bowl. Add brandy and stir well. Dough should be smooth and compact. Roll out on pastry cloth until dough is ½ inch thick. Cut with a round cookie cutter about 1 inch in diameter. Bake on a lightly greased cookie sheet at 375 degrees for 12 to 15 minutes, until lightly browned. Let cool. Dust with confectioners' sugar. Makes about 48 cookies.

Roscón de Reyes
(Holiday Bread)

1 package (1 tablespoon) dry yeast
  with 1 teaspoon water
¾ cup water
1 tablespoon orange flower water
  (often sold in Italian food shops)
  or strong tea
½ teaspoon grated lemon peel
6 cloves
½ cup butter
1 tablespoon lard or
  vegetable shortening

2 eggs; plus 1 egg, lightly beaten
1 tablespoon Spanish brandy
  or cognac
½ cup milk, scalded and cooled
5 cups all-purpose flour
Candied fruit slices
1½ tablespoons sugar, preferably
  coarse, for sprinkling
½ teaspoon salt
½ cup sugar

Dissolve yeast in ¼ cup warm water. Simmer ½ cup water with orange flower water or tea, lemon peel, and cloves for 10 minutes, covered. Let cool. Discard cloves.

Cream butter, lard, sugar, and salt in a bowl. Beat in 2 eggs. Add brandy, milk, water-and-lemon mixture, and softened yeast. Gradually mix in flour with a wooden spoon until dough is slightly soft and sticky. Knead on a floured working surface, adding more flour as needed, until smooth and elastic, about 5 minutes. Place dough in a greased bowl, turn to coat with oil, and cover with a towel. Place in a warm spot, such as an unlit oven, until doubled in size, about 2 hours. Punch down and knead again for 5 minutes. Insert a good-luck token, such as a coin or a miniature ceramic animal.

Shape dough into a large ring, pressing the ends together to seal. Place on a lightly greased cookie sheet. Decorate with fruit slices, pushing them slightly into the dough. Let ring rise in a warm spot for about 1 hour, or until double in size. Brush on egg beaten with water. Sprinkle with 1½ tablespoons sugar. Bake at 350 degrees for 35 to 40 minutes, or until a deep golden brown.

Buñuelos
(Cuban Puffs)

2 lbs. yucca
1 lb. sweet potatoes
½ lb. fresh pumpkin
2 eggs
2 teaspoons lard or vegetable shortening
6 ozs. butter

½ cup water
½ teaspoon anise
3 cups all-purpose flour
Vegetable oil for frying

Peel vegetables and cut into cubes. Boil in salted water until tender. Drain and let cool. Place vegetables into a blender. Add eggs, lard, and butter. Mix well. Set aside.

In a small saucepan over medium heat, reduce anise and ½ cup water to 2 tablespoons of liquid. Mix with vegetables. Gradually add flour until a dough is formed that does not stick to your hands.

Shape small logs from the dough, twisting each into the shape of an 8. Fry in vegetable oil until golden brown. Arrange on a plate and pour syrup over them (see below). May be eaten hot or cold. Makes about 24.

SYRUP

1 cup granulated sugar
1 cup water
1 4-inch cinnamon stick

1 teaspoon lemon juice
1 teaspoon orange flower water or
    strong tea

Put sugar and cinnamon stick in a small saucepan with 1 cup water. Heat together gently until sugar dissolves. Bring to a boil for a minute or two, until the liquid thickens slightly. Remove from heat, remove cinnamon stick, and stir in lemon juice and orange flower water.

Rice Pudding

½ cup short-grain rice, uncooked
1½ cups water
½ teaspoon salt
2 strips lemon peel
4 cups milk

1 cinnamon stick; ground cinnamon
    to taste
1 cup sugar
Combine rice, water, salt, and lemon

peel in a pot. Bring to a boil. Cook over low heat until rice is done, about 18 minutes. Remove lemon peel. In a separate pot, scald milk with cinnamon stick and add to cooked rice. Cook over low heat, stirring often with a wooden spoon. When mixture is creamy, add sugar and continue cooking for approximately 5 minutes. Remove from heat. Remove cinnamon stick. Pudding should be creamy and not too thick; it will thicken as it cools. Sprinkle with ground cinnamon. Serves 6.

Guava Cheesecake

CRUST

1½ cups graham cracker crumbs
¼ cup sugar
½ cup (1 stick) melted butter

In medium bowl combine cracker crumbs, sugar, and butter. Press mixture into lightly greased 9-inch springform pan; cover bottom and ½ inch up the side. Bake for 6 minutes at 375 degrees. Cool.

FILLING

2 16-oz. cans guava shells
32 ozs. cream cheese, softened
1¼ cups sugar
5 large eggs
¼ cup all-purpose flour
¼ teaspoon salt

Preheat oven to 325 degrees. Drain guava shells, saving syrup. Purée half of shells in a food processor, save other half for topping. In a large bowl or electric mixer, beat cream cheese until fluffy. Add sugar gradually. Add eggs one at a time, beating after each addition. Beat in remaining ingredients. Pour into crust. Bake for about 1 hour and 15 minutes. Turn oven off, open door slightly, and leave cake in oven for 30 minutes. Remove from oven and cool thoroughly.

GLAZE

1 cup guava syrup
2 teaspoons cornstarch
2 tablespoons sugar

Over low heat, boil syrup, cornstarch and sugar, blending to a smooth glaze. Cool. Arrange remaining half of guava shells on top and cover cake with glaze. Serve cold or at room temperature.

Bread Pudding

1 loaf Cuban bread
¼ lb. butter, cut into small pieces
3 large eggs
½ teaspoon salt
2 teaspoons vanilla extract
2 teaspoons almond extract
1 cup guava paste, cut into
 small pieces
2 or 3 large apples, peeled and
 cut into small pieces

1 16-oz. can fruit cocktail, drained
1 cup raisins
1 cup shelled almonds, skinned and
 chopped
1 5-oz. can evaporated milk
2 cups sugar
Pineapple slices, maraschino
 cherries, and sliced almonds,
 for garnish (optional)

Cut bread into slices about 3 inches thick and soak them in water for about 10 to 15 minutes. Squeeze water out of bread and place in a colander for a few minutes to continue draining. Place bread in a large mixing bowl and break into small pieces with your hands.

Add all remaining ingredients except garnishes. Mix well and turn into a large buttered baking pan, about 9 x 13. Bake at 350 degrees for 1½ to 2 hours, or until a toothpick inserted in center comes out clean. Remove from oven. (If desired, decorate with pineapple slices, cherries, and almonds for last 20 minutes of baking.) The guava paste gives the bread pudding a distinctive flavor. Serves 8–10.

Coffee Pudding

2 eggs
¼ cup sugar
1 teaspoon cocoa

⅛ teaspoon salt
1 cup milk
1 cup cold strong coffee

Beat eggs slightly. Add sugar, cocoa, salt, milk, and coffee. Pour into greased custard cups. Place in pan containing hot water about 1 inch deep. Bake in moderate oven 350 degrees for about 1 hour, or until firm. Serves 4.

Sopaipillas
(Mexican Fritters)

1 cup vegetable oil
Homemade pastry dough or 1 loaf frozen dough
1 cup honey

Roll dough out to a thin layer, cut into small triangles, and cut a slit through the center of each. Heat oil in a medium-sized skillet. Drop in dough triangles and keep turning them until they puff up and turn golden brown. Remove from skillet with a slotted spoon and drain on paper towels. May be served as bread or dessert. For dessert, drizzle honey on top before serving. Makes about 12 sopaipillas.

Bolitas
(Pecan Puffs)

½ cup unsalted butter
2 tablespoons sugar
1 teaspoon almond flavoring

1 cup cake flour
1 cup pecans, chopped
½ cup powdered sugar

Cream together butter, sugar, and almond flavoring. Stir flour and pecans into butter mixture. Roll into small balls and bake on cookie sheet for 25 minutes at 300 degrees. Roll in powdered sugar while still warm until well coated. Makes about 2 dozen.

Fruit Compote

¼ lb. dried prunes, chopped
¼ lb. dried apricots, chopped
1 14-oz. can crushed pineapple,
  drained
2 small cans mandarin oranges,
  drained

1 15-oz. can cherry pie filling
½–1 teaspoon cinnamon, to taste
¾–1 cup pecans or walnuts, chopped
1 cup sherry

Place prunes on bottom of a well-greased 2-quart casserole. Add apricots, pineapple, oranges, and cherries. Sprinkle with cinnamon and nuts evenly over the top, then pour sherry over all. Bake at 350 degrees until mixture bubbles. Serve warm or at room temperature. Serves 10–12.

Honey Teiglach

4 eggs, separated
1 teaspoon peanut oil
¾ cup matzoh cake meal
½ cup potato starch
Pinch of salt

1 lb. honey
¾ cup sugar
1 teaspoon ginger
½ cup water
½ cup nuts, finely chopped

Beat egg whites until peaks form. Beat yolks until creamy, add oil and salt, and keep beating until thick. Fold in egg whites. Sift cake meal, potato starch, and salt 4 times. Fold into eggs. Roll this dough into a long narrow piece and cut in 1-inch squares. Bring honey, sugar, ginger, and water to a boil in a large deep pan. Drop dough squares into this syrup. Boil over medium heat for 45 minutes. Place on a wet board and sprinkle with finely chopped nuts. Makes about 12.

Honey Cake

3 cups cake flour, sifted
2 teaspoons baking powder
½ teaspoon salt
1 cup butter
1 cup honey

4 eggs, well beaten
1 tablespoon lemon juice
1 teaspoon grated lemon rind
¾ cup nuts, chopped

Sift together flour, baking powder, and salt. Cream butter with honey. Blend in eggs, lemon juice, and lemon rind. Add to flour mixture. Blend smoothly. Mix in nuts. Pour into large loaf pan lined with greased paper. Bake at 350 degrees for 1 hour.

Sponge Cake

12 large eggs (room temperature)
Pinch of kosher salt
1½ cups sugar
3 tablespoons orange juice

1 tablespoon lemon juice
¾ cup matzoh cake meal
2 tablespoons potato starch
Vegetable oil

Separate egg yolks and whites, then beat whites with salt until they form peaks. Add sugar slowly to egg whites. Add egg yolks and citrus juices, and beat. Add cake meal and potato starch very slowly. Mix until batter is very smooth.

Grease an 8 x 12 inch pan with a small amount of vegetable oil and line with waxed paper. Pour batter into pan. Bake at 325 degrees for 20 minutes. Lower temperature to 300 degrees and bake for another 25 minutes. Cake is done when toothpick comes out clean. To cool, invert over dish towel on dining room chair!

Nut Sponge Cake

6 large eggs (room temperature)
Dash of kosher salt
1½ cups sugar
1 cup matzoh cake meal
½ cup potato starch

½ cup plus 1 tablespoon water
Rind and juice of 1 lemon or orange
¾ cup nuts, chopped
1 cup jelly or jam (for jelly roll version)

Separate eggs and beat whites with salt until foamy. Slowly add ¾ cup sugar. Beat until stiff. Set aside. Cream ¾ cup sugar with egg yolks until thick and yellow. Slowly add cake meal, potato starch, water, rind and lemon juice to the egg yolk mixture. Add nuts and mix well. Fold carefully into egg-white mixture; do not mix. Pour into large, ungreased tube pan. Bake at 325 degrees for about 1 hour, or until golden brown. Invert pan. The cake will not fall out of the pan. Cool completely, then cut out of pan.

This cake may be baked in a 10 x 15 inch jelly-roll pan (lined with waxed paper) at 325 degrees for 35 minutes. Turn onto a cloth sprinkled with sugar. Roll up cake with towel. Cool slightly, then unroll. Spread with 1 cup jelly or jam. Reroll and let cool.

Drinks

White Sangria

1 bottle dry white wine
1 bottle ginger ale or club soda
1 lemon, sliced
1 bunch seedless grapes (green and red)

1 orange, sliced
1 cup fresh strawberries, stemmed
Fresh mint for garnish

Pour wine and ginger ale in large pitcher, add fruit, and stir. Add ice cubes to chill. Serve in large wine goblets, garnish with fresh mint. Serves 12.

Ginger Grape Juice

2 whole cloves
½ small cinnamon stick
3 tablespoons lemon juice

3 tablespoons sugar
1 quart grape juice
2 cups ginger ale

Tie spices in cheesecloth. Combine lemon juice, sugar, and grape juice, and immerse spices. Cook over low heat for 15 minutes. Chill thoroughly. Just before serving, add ginger ale. Serve over ice. Serves 6–8.

Bog Cranberry Punch

2½ cups fresh cranberries
2 cups water
1 cup sugar
2 cups apple juice, chilled

1 cup cranberry juice
½ cup lemon juice, chilled
1 cup canned pineapple cubes
1 quart ginger ale, chilled

Combine cranberries, water, and sugar. Cook over low heat until tender. Strain and chill. Add cranberry mixture to remaining ingredients. Serve cold. Serves 18.

Eggnog

1 dozen eggs
2½ cups superfine sugar
2 cups Jamaica rum

1 cup peach brandy
1 quart milk
1 quart heavy cream

Separate eggs. Beat sugar into egg yolks. Slowly stir in liquors. Add milk. Beat heavy cream and fold in. Beat egg whites and fold in. Makes 15 8-oz. cups (serves 16–20).

Festival Punch

2 quarts ginger ale
1 quart fresh strawberries, stemmed
1 cup sliced bananas

2 cups pineapple juice
1 cup orange juice

Combine all ingredients. Serve over ice. Serves 12–16.

Christmas Punch

STEP 1

4 cups fresh cranberries
2 cups water
2 cups sugar

1 teaspoon gelatin
¼ cup boiling water
2 cups ginger ale

Cook the cranberries in 2 cups of water until they burst. Add sugar. Dissolve gelatin in ¼ cup boiling water. Mix all the above ingredients together and freeze in ice cube trays.

STEP 2

4 tea bags
4 cups boiling water
1 cup sugar

1½ cups orange juice
1⅓ cups lemon juice
1 pt. ginger ale, chilled

Steep tea bags in 4 cups boiling water. Add sugar, then juices. When ready to serve, whip frozen cranberry mixture in blender and add to punch. Add chilled ginger ale. Serves 16.

Hot Wine

1 liter cabernet sauvignon wine
1 teaspoon ground cloves
1 teaspoon nutmeg
1 teaspoon cardamom
½ cup prunes, chopped

½ cup raisins
1 teaspoon allspice
4 long strips orange peel
4 long strips lemon peel
1 cup Napoleon brandy
1 cup sugar

In a large pot, warm wine over low heat. Add sugar and rest of ingredients. Taste and add more sugar if desired. Serve in a large ceramic pitcher. Serves 8–10.

Don Gustavo's Last Nochebuena

My grandfather Gustavo Jimenez held the office of consul for Loyalist Spain in Ybor City, and he took great pride in his position. His office was in a building in downtown Tampa, and he dutifully made the daily trip on the Columbus Drive streetcar, which picked him up at the corner and delivered him, ten minutes later, at the front of his office building on Franklin Street. His habit was to put a nickel in the fare box and then hand the conductor a nickel tip. Some conductors took it, most didn't, but they all knew and respected the small, well-dressed Spaniard.

In spite of all the time spent at the office, it was at the house at 1019 Columbus Drive that most of my grandfather's consulate business was transacted. Our parlor and porch were always full of newly immigrated Spaniards. Some were fleeing the fierce civil war then raging in Spain, some were deserters from the International Brigades, and some were just coming to Tampa to work in the booming cigar factories of Ybor City. Life was never dull at Don Gustavo's house.

Gustavo Jimenez, the Spanish consul, in his office.

Don Gustavo had built a large, commodious dwelling to house his seven children, as well as a mechanic's garage nearby, to give the black sheep of the family, Uncle Paul, a place to make a living. By 1937, the year of the Last Christmas Tree, all had married and moved away except for Lola, my spinster aunt, and my mother, Consuelo. My mother and father, J.B. Pacheco, had elected to live in the big house with my grandparents while my brother, Joseph, and I were still small, until Dad saved up enough money for us to move into our own house.

My grandfather was accustomed to having money. He had lost a fortune fleeing Carranza's troops when they took Monterrey, Mexico, but he promptly remade the money in a series of breweries, bars, and related enterprises. He was a man of great culture and played the flute with distinction. He appreciated great art and read to us from the classics every chance he got, whenever he could catch us and get us to sit still.

His own children seemed to share his creative spark and his willingness to think big.

The year 1937 did not begin well, for the Great Depression was afoot. At our house we were used to the presence of gaunt transients at our back door, waiting for handouts and leftovers after each meal. To a ten-year-old who knew no other way, all of this seemed normal. I didn't know whether we were poor or rich, but you had to be brain-dead not to realize that it was better to be giving out leftovers than to be in line receiving them. As an abstract lesson, this translated roughly into "Better to give than to receive," and it was a lesson that would stick with me for the rest of my life.

On the all-important fighting front in Spain, our fortunes were waning. My grandfather and I would go up to his upstairs office and move the little red pins back, ever backward, on the map. The fighting in Teruel was going badly. Bilbao was all but lost, and even the staunch defenders of Madrid seemed about to cave in despite the exhortations of La Pasionaria, the voice of the Loyalist cause, who could still be heard on our powerful short-wave radio, emotionally shouting, "No pasaran!" (They shall not pass!). It looked like the end for the Loyalists of the Spanish Republic. They would not survive 1938.

Don Gustavo was a realist—not in the least bit pessimistic or fatalistic, but as he told his faithful wife, Carmen, he felt sure the Republic would fall, and when it did, he would die too. Carmen, a practical Gallego (Galician) and tough as nails, had survived much worse than the fall of Loyalist Spain, and she would put on her hard face when he spoke that way, scold him, and refuse to talk to him until he recanted. But still, Don Gustavo knew 1938 would bring the end.

So it was that the idea of constructing an elaborate Christmas display in the living room of 1019 Columbus Drive came from my grandfather Don Gustavo. We would build the biggest, most beautiful, most original, most fantastic Christmas display ever seen in Ybor City, and that would cheer everybody up.

It never took much to get the creative juices going in our family, so at Don Gustavo's suggestion, everyone began to gather at night and on the weekends to plan and construct the magnificent Christmas display stretching from one corner of the room to the other.

To begin with, instead of a single Christmas tree, there were *two* trees. The one in the right corner of the room was the bigger of the two, hung lavishly with silvery tinfoil strips, at the end of which hung gaily-colored crystal bulbs. This tree represented Christmas Past. As in the old country, real candles and elaborate, handmade ornaments, many of them family heirlooms, were fastened to the branches.

At the foot of this impressive tree, and also representing Christmas Past, was a magnificent nativity scene. The figures were exquisitely hand-carved, also heirlooms from Mexico and Spain. Carmela, Don Gustavo's oldest daughter, had married a Mexican Nationalist and so was allowed to remain in Mexico when the Revolutionary Army had expelled all other foreigners, including her parents, brothers, and sisters. She had saved many of the family treasures, including the nativity scene, which she had later sent to her family in Tampa.

At the center of the nativity scene stood the Christ Child's manger, Joseph, and Mary, surrounded by pairs of farm animals—sheep, cows, goats, and one donkey. The Three Wise Men approached on their camels. One of them was named Baltazar, which was my father's middle name, a fact that inexplicably always made me swell with pride. The entire nativity scene was surrounded by sand, and great care was taken to preserve biblical accuracy and the highest standard of realistic detail. Even the tiny electric light that served as a campfire was covered with crinkly red cellophane so as to more realistically simulate fire.

The entire scene was mounted on tables and chairs traveling the length of the room, making the display easy to see and the fineness of detail easy to appreciate. No table legs or chairs were left visible but were instead covered gracefully to resemble rolling hills and valleys.

In the other corner, to the left of the tableau, was the celebration of Christmas Present. Here there was a smaller tree strung with modern electric lights, and below it a huge, snow-covered mountain. Leading down from the mountain were long and curving roads, alongside which were scattered dozens of miniature houses, some with carports, and each one lit with a tiny electric bulb. Little people stood in their yards looking skyward. Fortunately, all of these trimmings were available at Kress, Woolworth, and other five-and-dime stores, and in spite of being excellently crafted, they did not cost a great deal, making it easy for us to populate our twentieth-century mountain with lots of houses and people.

It was my grandfather's idea that the contrast between Christmas Past and Christmas Present should be a telling one. That the modern tree was neither as large nor as elaborate as the nativity tree signified the diminished importance of Christ's birth to modern society in 1937. I doubt if anybody outside the family caught that symbolism, but it made Don Gustavo feel good that anyone with a brain might work out that bit of philosophical observation if he cared to.

Whereas the nativity tree had a bright, beautiful star of the East at its peak, the modern tree was topped by a replica of Lindbergh's Spirit of St. Louis monoplane. Held aloft between the two trees was one of the symbols of modern society's forgetfulness—Santa Claus, in his reindeer-led sleigh, about to dispatch presents to one and all—(this symbolism of course utterly lost on a ten-year-old whose head was filled with visions of toys and sweets).

Now came the *pièce de résistance*. My uncle Paul, the black sheep of the family and our resident wit and storyteller, had found an abandoned bathtub in a junkyard. He plugged the tub so that it wouldn't leak and nestled it snug between the two trees. Like the ancient river of Lethe in Hades, this boundary of forgetfulness would separate Christmas Past from Christmas Present.

Uncle Gus, a top salesman, inventive and full of the excitement of life, brought a dozen tiny boats, which zipped back and forth on the lake propelled by bits of sodium. Uncle Gus's flotilla also included candle boats, whose effect when the lights were turned off was magical.

Building a huge Christmas display is somewhat akin to writing a novel or a screenplay, or designing a house. All of the pieces do not occur to the creator at once, and most of the best touches are born spontaneously, after the project is well underway. Sometimes, in fact, it is just these accidents of creativity that prove to be the main attraction. So it is that I must now digress for a moment in order to relate just such an accident.

My father's brother John Pacheco was famous in Ybor City. As handsome and elegant as matinee idol John Barrymore, John owned an insurance company and was a prominent city politician. To be a politician in the corrupt city government of that period was to insure yourself of a healthy income.

I loved Uncle John, but I rarely saw him. When I did, I was always awed by the splendor of him. His clothes were beautifully tailored, and he seldom wore a hat, a habit which served to show off his beautiful hair, always perfectly groomed and combed. He was tall—a six-footer in a city of 5'4" men. He walked with an unrehearsed grace, and he was always smiling a little, as if enjoying some private joke or entertaining an amusing idea.

One day, in the midst of the construction of the giant Christmas display in our parlor, I saw Uncle John's gleaming Oldsmobile pull up outside. I ran out and he hoisted me up high in the air and twirled me 'round and 'round, like Lindbergh's Spirit of St. Louis. He smelled of lilac talc, a sure sign he'd been to Gaspar's Barber Shop on Nebraska and Palm.

My father, J.B., the baby of his family, was at work at the pharmaceutical warehouse where he was employed. Only my mother was there to greet Uncle John. My uncle had an impeccable, courtly, Old World manner with women, even his own sister-in-law. I couldn't help but notice that even my stoical mother often appeared flustered in my uncle's presence.

As Uncle John explained it to my stunned mother, he had been the beneficiary of a bit of good fortune and as a result had a bit of surplus cash. That he would mention this at all was in itself astounding, for the three Pacheco brothers were known to be close-mouthed about their finances. Nor did John choose to elaborate further. In the Ybor City of the depression years, a sudden windfall of cash usually meant the family had hit the number (*sacar la bolita*) or had received an unexpected inheritance. Of course, in Uncle John's case, deep in the pockets of Tampa's corrupt government, the answer was probably a bit more prosaic.

In any event, Uncle John then reached into his inside coat pocket and pulled out a Christmas card, which he gave to my mother. Once again he picked me up and gave me a kiss.

"Remember, Chelo, this money is only for the two boys, and it must *all* be spent on toys. Tell Baltazar I'll beat him up if I find out he's spent it on clothes or anything sensible. Let this be a Christmas to remember."

Uncle John was gone before my mother could open the Christmas card. I'll never forget the sight of that crisp fifty-dollar bill as it fluttered to the floor.

My mother put a hand to her mouth, and I let out a blood-curdling yell, waking up my brother, Joseph, who was sleeping on the couch.

"We're rich!" I shouted, bringing my grandmother, a butcher knife in her hand, from the kitchen. My *abuela* (grandmother) lived in perpetual fear that Carranza would one day appear in Ybor City and run the Spaniards out of their homes.

In 1937, fifty dollars could equip an entire football team—*and* a basket-ball team, *and* a baseball team! What was more, the money would allow us to connect Christmas Past to Christmas Present.

In the Maas Brothers toy department was a Lionel electric train, particularly expensive and beautifully detailed. It was operated and powered by two tiny black boxes. A light on the front of the engine lit the train's path as it sped down the track, emitting puffs of smoke and tooting its whistle. With it came a coal tender, passenger cars, and a platform car at the back, also lit with electric bulbs. It even had a tiny engineer, conductor, and passengers. *This* was a toy for adults, too good for kids to wreck. It cost $18.75, a princely sum in those days.

My Uncle Paul lay the tracks so that they ran in a circle around the tub of water. Then, in a stroke of genius, he built a tunnel *through* the center of the papier-mâché mountain, so that when all the lights were turned off, the lit train seemed to disappear into thin air, reappearing a few seconds later on the other side of the mountain, smoke puffing, whistle blowing. This was the big hit of our nightly shows—it caused grown men and women to applaud and children to cry with happiness. Word spread all over Ybor City, and even as far as the Anglo section of Palma Ceia, of our marvelous Christmas display.

Now, I don't want the reader to think I was an ungrateful child, but my more practical side took over at this point. My brother, Joseph, and I had been given fifty dollars. Yes, we had football helmets, a new catcher's mitt, and a new basketball, but a significant portion of the loot had been spent on an *adult* toy, from which we did not immediately benefit.

Feeling somewhat indignant, I asked for the money that was left over. I had a plan. Down at Woolworth's was the poor man's version of that opulent electric wonder of a train. Made of cheap tin, it had no electric power or fancy details, and it was powered by the winding of a hand spring. It was, moreover, not a replica of the beautiful steam-powered locomotives and their fancy passenger cars, but a cheap and simple replica of the sleek Silver Streak, which ran between Tampa and New York. For a few pennies more you could add extra track.

For days my brother and I played with nothing but our Silver Streak. We ran the tracks hither and yon, even building a railway bed outside. Boy, we were having a great time.

That year a representative of the Spanish government and his wife had been invited as special guests to our Nochebuena feast, along with scores of politicians. Don Victoriano Manteiga—a lector and the publisher of Ybor City's trilingual newspaper, *La Gaceta*—and all sorts of other dignitaries would also be in attendance.

Great was the hubbub at the big house, as an extra pig, two turkeys, and cases of wine and beer were delivered to the kitchen. It was on the afternoon of Nochebuena, when Uncle Paul came to test the electrical circuits and the ever-failing light bulbs one last time, that disaster struck.

The baby of the Jimenez clan was a wondrously good-looking, fresh-faced, fun-loving young man named Ferdie. I had been named after him, and he was very special to me, always treating me as if I were his son. Ferdie was an executive. In the manner of all executives, and never one to partake in physical labor, he sat in the corner looking on as we all added our finishing touches to the Christmas display. Everyone exclaimed and oohed and aahed over the tiny boats, the tunneled-out mountain, and the Lionel train. "The Spanish ambassador is going to be impressed," my father said with great pride.

But executives are so genetically constructed that they cannot ever leave well enough alone. And of all the members of the Jimenez family, only Ferdie had not ever had one original or creative idea. Suddenly he stood up and clapped his hands loudly.

The four Jimenez brothers in the 1930s (from left, Gus, Paul, Ferdie, and Guillermo).

"I got it!" he shouted excitedly. "The cherry on the cake! The topper!"

His father, Don Gustavo, groaned. He loved his beautiful baby son, but had no illusions as to his creative talents. Abuelita looked adoringly at her favorite son and said, "Dejen que Fernandito hable" (Let Ferdie speak). All eyes turned to the slim young man with the Frederic March profile.

"What if we had two trains running at the same time?"

My heart sank.

"We'll have them leave the station at the same time, one track a bit above the other. The Lionel will be on the inside track of the mountain, running along the rim of the lake. The other will arc above, and with a longer way to go, it will lose. Don't you see it? The past is the best, it beats the future!"

"Brilliant," said Abuelita, who probably hadn't understood a word Ferdie had said.

"A good trick, a good philosophical point," said Don Gustavo, impressed by the first original thought to come from the brain of his executive son.

"It's easy to set up," said Uncle Paul, taking me by the hand.

Of course, we were crushed. There went our train. My brother, Joseph, being a more sensitive, genius sort of kid, immediately threw up on the kitchen floor. He was sent to his room where he pulled down the shades, put a depressing Mahler symphony on the phonograph, and crawled into bed. He was very advanced for a young depressive. No one even noticed his gesture, and that in itself was exquisitely depressing.

Suffice it to say that Uncle Paul outdid himself. We rehearsed the race again and again. The Lionel beauty always won.

At six o'clock, the adults all went home to get dressed, and the servants worked alongside Abuelita, my mother, and Aunt Lola to prepare the perfect Nochebuena feast. Nochebuena 1937 would be the most memorable since Benito Juárez the dog had crashed through the door in Mexico and leaped into Uncle Paul's outstretched arms!

I dressed hurriedly and went downstairs to make sure the trains would run just right. After all, I was in charge of winding my Silver Streak. The Lionel ran on electricity, but mine had to be wound tight.

I cannot accurately recall the exact moment of my flash of brilliance, but when it hit me, I almost yelled Shazam! It was an idea so pure in concept, so easy to execute, and so stunning in effect that I was bowled over.

What if I disconnected the track of my Silver Streak just as the Lionel came out of the mountain? What if the entire Silver Streak train went arcing *over* the Lionel, just as it emerged, smoke puffing, whistle blowing, lights flashing in every car! What a spectacle! What a hit!

I grew excited imagining the tableau. What if I aimed the track so that the Silver Streak flew over the Lionel and *into the lake,* all six cars sinking to the bottom while the sodium boats putt-putted around and the candle boats floated serenely atop the Great Wreck of the Silver Streak? Why, folks would talk about it for years to come. It would become a legend in Ybor City. Stealthily I set about derailing my very own train.

Satisfied with the perfection of my plan, I went upstairs to await the arrival of our guests. My brother was hiding under a mountain of covers and pillows. He was listening to "The Gates of Kiev" and crying softly. I decided not to tell him about my planned wreck of the Silver Streak. What the heck, he was having fun his way, and I was going to have fun my way.

Finally, our guests arrived. Drinks and hors d'oeuvres were consumed, and then, with much fanfare, everyone gathered in front of the great Christmas display.

Working like a mad stage manager, Uncle Paul presented his light show to appreciative applause. The candle boats and putt-putts got polite cries of "Bravo!" and "Olé!"

But the big moment was drawing near. My grandfather got up and grandly announced the Race of the Silver Streak and the Lionel Special. Everyone chuckled and settled back to enjoy this little drama.

The race began. Uncle Ferdie yelled, "A quarter on the Lionel!" and people laughed. Down the backstretch of the bathtub lake they came, neck and neck. Right on schedule, the Lionel Special made its sudden disappearance into the mountain, and the Silver Streak climbed until it was just higher than the tunnel exit.

Abuelita, Joseph, cousin Junior, Ferdie, and Abuelo.

I wanted to close my eyes, but I couldn't. I had to see this. This was my creation, my contribution to the greatest Nochebuena display ever built! I held my breath. For a moment, everything seemed to stop. The Spirit of St. Louis stopped—the putt-putts, the candle boats—all of it stopped. Even the twinkling star of the East paused mid-twinkle.

The guests murmured as they saw the light in the tunnel. It was the Lionel Special, gaining speed, coming on, smoke puffing, whistle blowing, lights aglitter, and still neck and neck with the modern wonder train, the Silver Streak.

Suddenly the crowd gasped, and everyone held their breath. The Silver Streak had left the rails! It was airborne! It flew *over* the Lionel Special and landed with a splash in the lake, toppling every last putt-putt and candle boat.

There was a long, horrifying moment of silence as, open-mouthed, my entire family saw their masterpiece defamed. No one said a thing.

"Marvelous!" The Spanish envoy stood and applauded.

"Charming!" said his wife, a beautiful French lady.

"Muy bien hecho!" (Well done!) said the usually taciturn Don Victoriano Manteiga, clearing his throat.

Then they all stood, applauding, until Abuelita, fighting the urge to strangle me, turned on the lights and announced: "Nochebuena begins! A la mesa!" (To the table!).

How I survived that night I do not know. I ate hurriedly, feigned a wine-induced sleepiness, and was excused early. Everyone acted as though I was as innocent as a lamb. Only my Uncle Paul had that twinkle in his eye that told me he had been there many times. Undoubtedly, it made him reflect on how times had changed in his father's house. For less than that, he'd have been hung by his thumbs in the cellar at Monterrey. He winked as I went by.

My grandfather was proven right. Spain's Loyalist government fell in 1938, and with its end he ran out of causes and breath at the same time. Abuelo died at the end of 1938, fulfilling his prophecy.

He was right about another thing. It wasn't the last Christmas tree for the Jimenez family, but no one doubted for a moment that it was the biggest, the most beautiful, the most original, and most fantastic Christmas display that had ever been seen in Ybor City.

Bibliography

Boni, Ada. *Italian Regional Cooking*. New York: Bonanza Books, n.d.

Casas, Penelope. *The Foods and Wines of Spain*. New York: Alfred Knopf, 1984.

Esposito, Mary Ann. *Celebration Italian Style*. New York: Hearst, 1995.

Goldsmith, Terence. *Christmas*. Poole, Dorset: Blanford Press, 1978.

Gonzmart, Adela, and Ferdie Pacheco. *The Columbia Restaurant Cookbook*. Gainesville: University Press of Florida, 1995.

Hazan, Marcella. *More Classic Italian Cooking*. New York: Alfred Knopf, 1978.

Lyons, Molly David Bar. *Jewish Cooking for Pleasure*. London: Paul Hamlyn, 1965.

Maestas, Margo. *Right Out of Margo's Kitchen*. Wheatridge, Col.: privately published, 1989.

Mussoletto, Ana. *The Art of Sicilian Cooking*. New York: Germany Publishing Co., 1971.

Nathan, Joan. *The Jewish Holiday Kitchen*. New York: Schocken Books, 1979.

Polvay, Marina. *Slim and Healthy Italian Cooking*. Surfside, Fla.: Surfside Publishing, 1990.

Poole, Shona Crawford. *The Christmas Cookbook*. New York: Atheneum, 1979.

Walker, Ann, and Larry Walker. *A Season in Spain*. New York: Simon and Schuster, 1992.

Credits

The recipes from *The Foods and Wines of Spain*, by Penelope Casas (New York: Alfred Knopf, 1984), *A Season in Spain*, by Larry and Ann Walker (New York: Simon and Schuster, 1992), and *The Christmas Cookbook*, by Shona Crawford Poole (New York: Atheneum, 1979) are reprinted in this volume by permission of the publishers.

Grateful acknowledgment is extended to the following people for contributing their recipes: Buster Agliano, Mary Alessi, Fifa Ciaccio, Kit Crowell, Bernadette Cunningham, Marie Cusmano, Vera Dubson, Teresa Fernandez, Kathi and David Gomendi, Adela Hernandez Gonzmart, Inocencia Galindo, Katie Galindo, Rosalie Irene, Jallele, Teresa Kaplan, Lottie Kimball, Natalie Kleinberg, Frances Leiderman, Margo Maestas, Consuelo Mafalda, Barbara Manning, Pamela McLaughlin, Marabel Morgan, Luisita Pacheco, Mariano Parra, Ermanno Perrotti, Marina Polvay, Tony Rametta, Francesco and Maria Rametta, Ana Torres, and Pauline Winick.

Index